A Woman's Guide
to Starting Her Own Business

A Woman's Guide to Starting Her Own Business

Turning Talent Into Profits

Cynthia S. Smith

A Citadel Press Book
Published by Carol Publishing Group

A Citadel Press Book
Published by Carol Publishing Group

Citadel Press is a registered trademark of Carol Communications, Inc.
Editorial Offices: 600 Madison Avenue, New York, N.Y. 10022
Sales and Distribution Offices: 120 Enterprise Avenue, Secaucus, N.J. 07094
In Canada: Canadian Manda Group, P.O. Box 920, Station U, Toronto, Ontario M8Z 5P9
Queries regarding rights and permissions should be addressed to Carol Publishing Group, 600 Madison Avenue, New York, N.Y. 10022

Carol Publishing Group books are available at special discounts for bulk purchases, sales promotions, fund raising, or educational purposes. Special editions can be created to specifications. For details, contact Special Sales Department, Carol Publishing Group, 120 Enterprise Avenue, Secaucus, N.J. 07094

Manufactured in the United States of America

10 9 8 7 6 5 4 3 2 1

Library of Congress Cataloging-in-Publication Data

Smith, Cynthia S.
   A woman's guide to starting her own business : turning talent into profits / by Cynthia Smith.
      p.   cm.
   "A Citadel Press book."
   ISBN 0-8065-1568-6 (pbk.)
   1. New business enterprises.   2. Women-owned business enterprises—Management.   I. Title.
HD62.5.S6248   1994
658.1'41—dc20   94-20354
                                     CIP

Thanks to Hillary S. Pannier for the astute suggestions that helped me write this book, and to Fred Pannier for the invaluable computer guidance that helped me produce it.

In battle or business, whatever the game,
In law or in love, it is ever the same;
In the struggle for power, or the scramble for pelf,
Let this be your motto—Rely on yourself.
For whether the prize be a ribbon or throne,
The victor is he who can go it alone.

THE GAME OF LIFE
John Godfrey Saxe, 1816–1887

Contents

A Woman's Guide
to Starting Her Own Business

1

The Whys of Working for Yourself

Wouldn't you love to have your own business, an enterprise that **you alone** created and built, that gives you freedom no job can offer, that can produce financial security for you and your family? You can do it. All you need is intelligence, energy, and this book.

I have created and taught courses at New York University and the University of Connecticut, one for people who wish to start businesses and one for women only. Why a different course for women? Because we are different; women have unique skills and expertise that are innate and special fears and attitudes that are societally imposed.

Women today have more complicated and demanding lives than men. As always, we have the responsibility of running the home, but now we're also involved with making money to maintain that home. Having a job may fill the family's financial needs, but it often doesn't fill a woman's special life needs. In many cases, having your own business is the best way to build a better life as well as a secure future for you and your family.

There are motivations other than financial ones for a woman to have her own job, career, profession. Emotional needs can be equally compelling. If you picked up this book, then you have reasons to want to go out and work for yourself.

Which of These Seven Scenarios for Starting a Business Applies to You?

1. *Honey, the Kids Have Shrunk Me.* You're at home with small children. Sure you're happy, but not totally. Being bereft of adult conversation has reduced your vocabulary to twenty-five words, all of them involving toilet training or threats. Maybe the mindlessness required to dust, scrub, wash, iron, and cook day after day is making you wonder if you've gone brain dead. You long for mental stimulation. You would love to go to work but worry about who would take care of the kids and home.

2. *The Coming College Crunch.* The kids are adorable and bright, and you lie awake nights wondering how you'll ever afford to give them the college education they deserve.

3. *The Empty Nest.* Your children have now grown and flown, and you are the abandoned custodian of an empty nest. You need a new life purpose. You've helped them achieve their potentials; now it's time to fulfill yours.

4. *The Lost-Job Contingency.* What would happen if your husband lost his job? You may have put aside some money, but in today's economy it could conceivably take him months, if not years, to find another job. Deep down, you are living with the fear that any long-term stoppage of your family's sole income could result in losing your home and life savings.

5. *The Dreaded Male Menopause.* You have just been told by your mate of thirty years that he's getting a hair transplant in preparation for his new life with a twenty-eight-year-old aerobics instructor. Or maybe this happened to the woman next door and you're getting nervous when you realize that you could not possibly maintain your lifestyle without your husband's paycheck. Should he walk out, or die, how would you support yourself and what would you do with the rest of your life?

6. *Retirement and Twenty-four-Hours-a-Day Togetherness.* Your husband is the faithful homebody type and plans to be faithfully at home for breakfast, lunch, and dinner as soon as he retires next year. You've been worrying that you may need an activity to get you out of the house before you go out of your mind.

7. *You Have a Job, But You're Not Happy.* The pay is poor, the future is nil, and you want something better. Or you have a family plus a full-time job and are living the treadmill existence of a gerbil; leave the house at seven, return at six, shop and cook on weekends. If you have small children, it's the nightmare of day care arrangements. If you have bigger kids, it means seeing them by appointment only.

Do any of these situations sound like yours? Are you dissatisfied with your life now and worried about your future? What it all comes down to is every woman's need for independence. No one should allow herself to be placed in the high-risk position of total reliance upon anyone. Relationships are not permanent. Marriage contracts carry no guarantees, and men are not immortal. Under all conditions, it will be a happier, more secure you when you have another vital, remunerative role in life besides that of homemaker.

If any of these scenarios fits you, it's time to think of going into your own business.

The Beauty and Benefits of Starting Your Own Business

It's all yours—your creation, your baby—and you alone reap all the benefits. Building a business is truly a heady experience (I should know, I've started three and have been my own boss for years). It offers the stimulation of a job and the satisfaction of direct-to-you compensation commensurate with your labors. Unlike working for someone else, where your competence and dedication produce profit for a corporate entity, in your own business you are the sole beneficiary of the fruits of your brain and labor.

No one gives you orders. No one tells you what to do and yells if you don't do it. You do not have to deal with a cantankerous and sometimes unreasonable superior. The only person you have to please is *you*. You make the decisions. Your time is your own. You can arrange your hours to suit your needs and the demands of your life—within reason, of course. That doesn't mean you close the place when you have a tennis game. But when there is a slow period, which occurs in all work, you can take off, providing the business is covered by an employee or an answering machine.

Think of the advantages in terms of everyday convenience. There are none of the hassles or expense of commuting, because you have the option of establishing a location nearby. Or better still, work at home, which cuts down on your initial risk investment, increases your profit margins, and gives you bona fide tax benefits.

The satisfactions can be enormous. A business is *your* personal production; developing it, making it grow into something real and solid, can be fantastically rewarding, both to your ego and your pocketbook.

The idea is exciting. Perhaps you have thought of it before but are a bit scared. After all, what do you really know about the intricacies of business? How do you know where to go for the products and services needed? Can you cope with the multiple facets of management—all the details and decisions that must be handled?

Of course you can. Do you realize that you are a highly experienced entrepreneur right now? You started up and are running the most complicated enterprise imaginable. The establishment of which you are CEO is called The Home. Just think about it. You are constantly involved in purchasing, accounting, scheduling, programming, personnel problems, distribution . . . the gamut of procedures that are part of everyday business management.

How different do you think these responsibilities are from those involved in the running of a company? True, there are certain disciplines, terminologies, and elements that are different, but your unique experience and training qualifies you to handle the most rigorous demands of a business. For anyone who has managed to get children off to school; arranged the complex logistics of lessons, medical, and dental appointments; marketed for, planned, and prepared meals; handled household equipment breakdowns and fought with repairmen; sold family cars and old houses, and bought new ones; is accustomed to working a solid twelve-hour day and being the fulcrum of a family—for such a person running a business might seem like a vacation. You already have the experience of heading a complicated organization. All you need is the technical information on how to convert this training into commercial expertise. I guarantee that by the time you have finished this book, you will be totally qualified to start and run your own business. So relax and read on. Everything you need to know about starting and operating a business is here.

Why Women Are Especially Suited for Small Business

A small business operates on a personal level. It has to; the limited size of the quarters and staff dictates the need for close relationships. This necessarily intimate set-up is tailor-made for the life skills of women because we are better than men at dealing with relationships and handling people.

There have been a spate of books on the differences between male and female business management; the contrasts in styles of leadership point up the greater suitability of women for small business. In a 1990 *Harvard Business Review* article called "The Way Women Lead," by Judy B. Rosener, men were described as preferring a "command and control" style in dealing with subordinates, relying on giving orders and appealing to self-interest.

That sort of approach is tough to put across when the boss is standing shoulder-to-shoulder with employees while packing products, shoving mailers in envelopes, or doing any of the down-and-dirty chores everyone has to perform when a business is just starting. Women, on the other hand, "prefer to work interactively," sharing power and information. They know instinctively how to get people to work with and for them while still maintaining a friendly relationship.

In her book *The Female Advantage*, Sally Helgesen claims that while men are hierarchical and interested in power for power's sake, women are intuitive and not interested in setting up those authority structures that men so adore. Cokie Roberts, the ABC News correspondent, joked that she could think of no better preparation for covering Congress than motherhood. "They all act like two-year-olds," she explained. When *Time* did a cover story a few years ago on the preponderance of successful female-founded small businesses, they noted women's different methods of leadership. "Men control by creating competition, women control by engendering cooperation." Engendering employee infighting might work constructively in a big company, but in a small business, it only creates chaos.

The classic male method of attacking a situation is instant, vigorous action. *The American Heritage Dictionary* defines "vigorous" as being a synonym of "active," implying "manly capacity to act with healthy strength and firmness." Women, on the other hand, tend to approach a problem with a flexible mindset that involves consideration of alternate solutions. In her 1982 book *In a Different Light: Psychological Theory and Women's Development*, Harvard psychologist Carol Gilligan presented this problem to two bright eleven-year-olds, Jake and Amy: What should a poor man do if his wife was dying and he could not afford to buy her medicine? Jake thought the man should steal the medicine and assume he would be able to convince a judge he had done the right thing. Amy thought he should find another way—maybe borrow the money or try to appeal to the pharmacist—because she felt stealing might cause the poor man even worse trouble. What if he went to jail, which would mean his wife would then never be able to get any more of the drug, and then who would take care of the poor woman?

Jake's self-confident, brash, "typically male" solution out-ranked Amy's "typically female" one on the rating scale of psychologists. But in the operation of a small business, the woman's way of reasoning through a problem and considering alternate solutions would be infinitely more effective.

In a large corporation, executives must often make fast decisions, but these are based upon pertinent information supplied to them by subordinates, as well as records of past results in similar situations. Also, few of these decisions are earth-shaking; only in rare situations can one individual's wrong turn wreak havoc. But in a small business, especially a start-up, there are no subordinates or history to guide or help. Each problem must be evaluated carefully; you cannot afford to act rashly since there is always the risk that a bad decision can destroy the company. The "female" approach of considering all sides and possibilities before jumping into action that could prove disastrous may not rate high on the machismo scale, but it is ideal for the demands of starting and building a successful enterprise.

Perhaps that's why today two out of every three businesses beginning with just one person are being started by women. According to Martha Firestone, vice president of the American Woman's Economic Development Corporation, this is the result of women having less of a chance to make it to the top of big companies, where only three percent of female employees reach top management status. But it is also the result of the many single mothers who, struggling to make ends meet, are driven to tap ability and drive they never knew they possessed.

I interviewed many women for this book, women who started from nothing and made it. In each case, the woman's goal was not only to achieve personal success, but to ensure the happiness and security of her family.

Men start businesses for money, power, and ego gratification. While doing research for this book, I have learned that women build businesses with the aim of providing a better life for their families. Women are the nurturers. Yes, they take justifiable pride in their successes, but they revel in the happiness and security their enterprises have brought to their families.

Achieving success was not easy for these women. Each one of them ignored and overcame the "you'll never make it" warnings usually issued to females by the gloom-'n'-doom boys from the banking and business worlds. Each had the guts to take risks, the self-confidence that she would make it no matter what the odds, and the willingness to work her fanny off to make a go of it.

A small business demands handling dozens of crises, decisions, and details, just like those you encounter daily in managing your home and the activities of your family. You see, you actually *are* an entrepreneur, only you didn't know it!

2

Know Before You Go: The Demands of Being in Business

Now that you've been whipped into a heady state about the glories of being your own boss, it's time to inject some sober notes of reality to prepare you for the downside. Of course, you knew there had to be some hardships because we've all been brought up on such homespun homilies as "There's no such thing as a free lunch" and "You don't get nuthin' for nuthin'."

There's a price to be paid for the privilege of becoming the owner of a profitable business, and I'm not just talking dollars and cents, but believe me, it's worth it. I have been an employee in a top executive position, and I have built and run my own business. Although there are times when I think back longingly to those days when the paycheck came regularly every Friday and the weekends were my own, I could never go back to working for anyone else but me. The marvelous freedom, the deep satisfaction, and the highly improved income have hooked me forever, as it will you. But you will be better equipped to weather the rough times if you are aware of the incipient problems now and can either learn to meet them head-on or, even better, stave them off entirely.

Family Resentment

If you have a husband and children, they will frequently be forced to do without you and your services, and if they resent the deprivation, you will suffer. You may no longer be home for all meals and available for chauffeuring the kids around; if they've been used to elaborate home-cooked meals every night, take-out foods, pizza, and the microwave may be a shock. You must prepare them for the changes that will occur in their lives and give them a darned good explanation for turning their world upside-down. When you've made up your mind to embark on a business venture, it's a good idea to sit the family down and discuss what it will entail for all of you. There will be a massive drain on your energies and emotions because you must put your heart, soul, and ego into the effort if your business is to succeed.

When they understand why this new activity is important to you, and how it fits into your blueprint for the family's future, you should be able to enlist their support and cooperation.

As the business gets going, try to involve them as much as possible. Once they become participants, in whatever way, they develop a proprietary feeling about "our business" and a sense of pride in being part of its growth. I've seen children helping out in stores and being delightful salesfolk; I remember my ten-year-old daughter proudly referring to "our clients." And I have seen hundreds of cases where resentful husbands turned into active partners once they saw the fun and profit in having one's own business.

I addressed the annual convention of the National Needle-work Association some years ago in Atlanta and was pleased to see a huge audience of women needlepoint-store owners accompanied by their husband and partners. The women's movement had aroused the consciousness of heretofore-housewives across the country who decided to break out of the kitchen and into the business world. A typical scenario involved a skeptical husband who reluctantly gave in to his wife's desire to start a shop, figuring it was better to finance her than have to face her depression at dinner every evening. Since needlepoint was something she knew, opening a store that sold kits and supplies along with instruction seemed a sensible enterprise. To everyone's surprise but hers, the store took off, and the husband developed the habit of dropping in and helping out on Saturdays. As the store began to prosper, he who had worked for someone else all his life began to see the pleasure and profit potential of independent proprietorship. At that point, he quit his job to join his wife full-time, taking over the administrative and financial details.

This allowed his wife to devote herself fully to creative management, for which she had displayed obvious talent by building up a large and growing customer base. The role-switch in their relationship and the added dimension of working together revitalized their marriage by turning it into a new, exciting partnership.

All Work and No Pay

Resign yourself to at least a year of no income from the business—just outgo. One of the facts of new business life is that all money must be constantly reinvested in the business until it shows a profit, which could take months or years. Unlike a job, where the wage scale is usually determined by the amount of labor demanded, your own business works in the reverse: you work endless hours and get paid nothing. The difference is that you know all this is only temporary and you have a goal. You are making an investment with a big possible payoff. You are putting in sweat-equity, and when the business has begun to turn a profit, you not only will be able to draw a good income, but will be the proud owner of a valuable property.

Dealing With Rejection

You had better learn to develop a tough hide to survive the rejections you will face from banks, suppliers, vendors, prospective customers, and many others along the way. You will learn to accept rebuffs and disrespect as merely the costs of doing business.

In spite of the fact that "we've come a long way, baby," the macho mystique is still alive and active out there and there will be men who won't treat you seriously or fairly just because you are female. My husband and I had our own advertising agency for twenty-five years, and although I was the copywriter and contact person and he was the graphic designer, there were many clients I never called upon without him. When I asked a question, the client answered him. There are still many men who find it difficult to relate to a woman as a peer or worse, a superior. When they call me "dear," I have a strong desire to respond with "yes, darling" and a kick in the groin. However, if the guy is a client or someone in a position to help my business, I just figure he suffers from a mental handicap that he has to live with and I'm only visiting.

Don't get paranoid when you encounter rejection. Be brutally self-honest and analytical: Is it perhaps your service or product rather than your gender in which he has no confidence? Could it be that your approach is wrong or your presentation is wanting? Placing instant blame for a failed transaction on bias may do great things for your self-esteem but it will not help your business.

Worry and Weariness

There will be sleepless nights when you worry about cash flow and how to pay your bills when your customers don't pay theirs. And when you fall into bed after one of those eighteen-hour-days, you may long to chuck the whole thing and get a job as a typist whose hands and mind stop work at 5 PM. Just keep telling yourself "it's only temporary—this too shall pass." Every one of the women whose success stories you will read about at the end of this book has undergone all these travails and has overcome them. As you will see from their stories, they had to be tough, they had to be persistent, they had to have a strong will to succeed, and they had to maintain such unshakable belief in their projects, that the possibility of failure was out of the question.

My intention here is not to discourage you from going into business but rather to encourage you to examine the realities of whatever choice you make to be certain it is the right one for you.

Let's Get Real

Do you have romanticized images of dashing about in designer suits while wheeling and dealing with suave Armani-clad men? If so, starting a small business, which will more likely involve wearing sweaters and jeans as you haggle with bristle-bearded slobs in synthetic slacks, can only lead to a let-down. Dreams of a glamorous future are fine, but making grandiose plans before you've even gotten off the ground is an impractical delusion.

Some years ago I created and taught a course called "How to Start a Business" in the Continuing Education for Women Division of the University of Connecticut. It was the early days of the women's movement, and I felt impelled to impart what I had learned—the gritty hard way—to women who may not have been as lucky as I to have been born with the advantages of tremendous self-confidence and an inability to accept the word "impossible."

The first day of the class, I asked each student what kind of business she planned to start. When two of the women announced they intended to open a coffee bean shop in Westport, I commended them on the concept. Then one of the pair asked if I was going to teach the class how to develop a franchised chain. I pointed out that such planning was a little premature since the store was as yet far from a reality and they did not have even one location. Then the other one mentioned they would miss the next few sessions because they were going to South America on a buying trip, blithely adding that it would be especially marvelous because the entire excursion would be tax-deductible. They were stunned when I asked, "Deductible from what?"

My idealism was sorely tried as I came to realize that most of the women were there not because they truly wanted to break out of a lifetime of consignment to women's limited roles, but because they were ashamed of their answer to the question "What do *you* do?" which was suddenly being asked of women at Connecticut dinner parties. Now instead of giving the unfashionable response, "I'm a housewife," they could make the impressive response, "I'm starting a business." In actuality, not one of them was ready to trade her bridge games and trips to the Bahamas for the dedication required to start a business.

Are *you*? Just to be sure that you know exactly what you will be getting into, let me point out the deprivations and difficulties you may have to undergo when you start different kinds of businesses.

The Demands of Specific Businesses

Now that you know all the *general* drawbacks to starting a business, let's get into the specific ones of various types of businesses. Before you decide what kind of business is for you, you should be aware of the requirements of that enterprise and be thoroughly prepared to deal with them. To plunge into a start-up situation without full knowledge of what you will be facing can be disastrous.

Retailing

A shop sounds like fun. Maybe you see it as somewhat social, with people dropping in to discuss their needs and turning to you for advice on making suitable selections. Not to mention the pleasure you will have when purchasing merchandise for the store and the satisfaction of seeing your excellent taste confirmed by favorable customer buying reaction. Wonderful. Just don't forget that your body has to be in that store, day and evening, plus Saturday and often Sunday, too. The sun may be out but you're in. Your pals are basking on the beach or having a great time on the golf course. You are in the store. Your husband doesn't work weekends, but you do, which means all those fun things you used to do together are no longer possible.

Sure you can hire help, but that cuts into the profits, and when you've just opened and customer traffic is only starting to build, every nickel counts. Employees can impose a heavy tariff and I don't mean only wages. There's that one-for-me, one-for-you approach to the cash register; even with computerization, it's hard to be sure every sale is recorded and every dollar goes into the till and not their pockets. It sounds like stealing, and it is, but you'd be surprised at how many retail employees regard this little activity as a perk of the job, equivalent to office workers taking home stationery, pens, and sundry office supplies.

And then there's the cost of their "who cares?" attitude toward customers. One of your major assets in a store is the goodwill created by customers' positive shopping experiences. Pleasant ambiance, helpful salespeople, and concerned management are as important as desirable merchandise and good pricing in bringing people back. How many times have you encountered surly or uncooperative sales clerks and vowed you would never patronize that store again? Unfortunately, few salespeople seem to be aware that their continued employment is directly related to the number of happy customers, so their demeanor and attitude directly affect not just the boss's future but their own as well. It's *your* business, so you will kill yourself to please every customer, because you know the success of your store depends on building a clientele that returns and recommends. Can you afford to leave this important work to an employee?

Another downer is boredom. Next time you are out shopping midmorning or midafternoon, peek into small stores and notice how many have a lone person sitting behind the counter. If she's staring into space idly, she's most likely an employee. If she has a frozen smile on her face and slight panic in her eyes, it's probably the owner wondering if that last customer was indeed her last. Remember that you're not Bloomingdale's, with people rushing in and out all day. There will be long lulls and hours of not seeing or speaking to a soul. Unfortunately, you cannot put a sign on the door saying "gone fishing" when things are slow, because once people find a shop closed at unexpected times, they will lose confidence in the place as a buying resource and will brand it as unreliable.

But take heart; all this doesn't go on forever. Once the business is established and profitable, the busy times will bring in enough sales to cover the slow times. Eventually you will be able to hire higher-level managerial help whom you can trust, and you will be free to come and go as you please.

Manufacturing

Producing an item which you have created imposes tremendous responsibilities. It requires research to learn where to obtain necessary components at the best possible terms, as well as how to arrange for packaging, shipping, and warehousing. Does the product involve legal regulations? Food products require specific manufacturing conditions; electrical products require approvals and conformity with codes. None of this is difficult; it merely takes time and systematic detailing of procedures.

Working at Home

It certainly is easier physically, but not always mentally and emotionally, to work out of home. The kids often do not take your need for privacy seriously and come barging in constantly. You're there, so why aren't you available? There's more personal discipline required when you want to work on the business but are drawn to homemaking needs. It takes determination to set up and keep firm business hours in a room that's next to the kitchen. It's OK and handy to run in and out periodically to baste the turkey. But if you're into elaborate cooking, you should not attempt to run a business with a phone squeezed between your neck and shoulder, talking to customers while you mince garlic and shallots. They may not be able to see or smell you, but they will surely be able to sense the distraction in your voice.

Another problem can be the neighbors. With the current growth of home businesses, residents are becoming aware, and frequently resentful, of the existence of a commercial venture in their residential neighborhoods. Backed by the probable existence of restrictive zoning laws, they are entitled to object. However, if your business does not bring in noticeably heavy traffic of people or vehicles that can pose hazards to playing children, or annoy people who want peaceful, quiet streets, chances are the neighbors will not complain or even notice. One of my students told me that when she moved into her new home a few years ago with intentions of setting up a cooking school in her kitchen, she was a bit apprehensive. But the very first morning she awoke to the sound of a crowing rooster from next door and realized her neighbor was illegally raising chickens in his garage. She smiled with relief and stopped worrying. No one has ever bothered her.

Every Business

Accept the fact that for the first year your business will demand total personal commitment. Getting it off the ground will take all of your time, thought, and energy. Crises will crop up constantly and you will seem to be putting out fires all the time. A car manufacturer that comes out with a new model fully expects it will take a year for their engineers to iron out unpredicted flaws and get rid of all the bugs. That's what you will be doing—alone. There will be days when you will become a firm believer in Murphy's Law, which states that anything that can go wrong will go wrong. For instance, you have a restaurant and the chef quits on Friday evening after hurling a cleaver at one of the waiters, which means you don his toque and apron and quickly print an abbreviated menu. Or you manufacture cheese balls and get a frantic call from a star customer who received a gross of cheddar when he had ordered Neufchâtel and you have to arrange for costly Federal Express replacement shipments. Or you are running a special event and learn that your bus drivers went out on a wildcat strike, and you have one hour to replace them.

There will be "those days," but you will soon learn to take them in your stride and adopt the motto that I had my daughter repeat whenever she went into a temper tantrum: "Panic is the enemy of efficiency." It worked every time. When she was little, just saying the big words quieted her; when she got older, the sense of the statement had a calming effect. Once the "shakedown" year is over and things are moving right along, you will look around and proudly survey the smoothly running operation you have created and be filled with the exhilaration of justifiable pride in your achievement.

3

Business Demeanor: How to Come Across as a Pro

"A man says what he knows, a woman says what will please." These words, written in the 1700s by Rousseau, illustrate a difference between the sexes that has been perpetuated by the way our mothers train us, with added support from *Cosmo*. A woman must be understanding, tactful, and cajoling. If she veers from this kinder, gentler path, she's pilloried like Hillary and mocked as a ball-breaker.

Let them say what they want. To operate successfully in the business world—a man's world—you had better sharpen your edges and drop the role of Ms. Nice Guy. This sweetness-and-light, sugar-and-spice girlie thing is not genetic, it's sociologic. You can change. In business, the goal is not be loved but to be taken seriously and respected. It is important that you become aware of how you deal with people, in order to avoid pitfalls that can impair your efficiency and effectiveness.

Business Behavior No-No's

Excuses, Excuses

"My dishwasher broke last night—wouldn't you know it?—just when I had a load of dishes and my warranty period is over. I have to wait at home all day for the repairman. He can't tell me exactly when he's coming—you know these service places—so I won't be able to come in to work today."

"Laurie was up all night vomiting. Who knows what junk she ate in school yesterday, or maybe she has a virus but she has no temperature. Anyway, I thought I'd keep her home from school—she's so exhausted—so I won't be able to come in to work today."

Whenever the phone rang at 8 AM, I knew it was Sally, the woman I had made the mistake of hiring to do part-time work in my office even though she had never worked in one. I would sigh as I picked up the phone, steeling myself for her litany of domestic woes. She knew how to handle our computer, she was pleasant to callers, and she filed intelligently, but she didn't have a clue about professional, business-like demeanor.

Unlike volunteer work, where no one dares make strong claims on your time because you're not getting paid and commitments are casual because there's no salary to insure obligation, business demands total dependability and regards time as money. Sally's behavior branded her as an unreliable amateur who could not be taken seriously, and she was eventually fired. What did she do wrong?

When you make a business call, be all business. No one has the time or interest to listen to the intimate details of your family life. All Sally had to say was: "I can't come in today. Is it all right if I come in tomorrow instead?" I would have either said yes or we would have arranged for another day, and the call would be completed in two minutes. Instead, I had to waste my precious time hearing domestic drivel that her mother might find fascinating, but I regarded as totally irrelevant I didn't want explanations; there was no need for excuses. She worked part-time and if she needed to rearrange her twenty-hours-a-week occasionally, it was no big deal.

Another cardinal business sin she committed was making me aware that her priorities were not in my favor. She was foolish enough to tell me that she put a household repair and her need to stay home with a not-too-sick child ahead of her obligations to her job. What she conveyed to me with her unnecessary explanations was that she was an unreliable employee who obviously did not understand that casual absences could not be tolerated when other people depend upon you.

Casual Commitment

Women who manage volunteer staffs tell me it's hell to keep track of scheduling because volunteers work when it suits their time frames, and cancel when something more interesting comes along. This creates a disregard for time and a disrespect for commitments—bad habits that do not translate well into the commercial world. She tells me that their cancellation calls are an entertainment in themselves, if you have the time to listen. For some reason, most likely guilt, their excuses are given in elaborate detail. She has heard the minutiae of ramifications of illnesses, failing body functions, and assorted ailments of close relatives who need immediate attention. And she has had her fill of household emergencies, malfunctioning equipment, overflowing septic tanks—all told in more detail than she cares to hear. Apparently the longer the explanation, the greater the volunteer's feeling of justification.

If this has been your life, you had better be prepared to alter your mindset. Going to work when you must is very different from going to work when you feel like it. Embarking upon a project such as starting a business is a serious endeavor that involves big money, other people, and other businesses, and cannot be handled like a hobby. Obligations are binding and commitments are just that—commitments. Time is a valuable commodity, and you must learn to control it carefully.

Telephone Technique

Suppose you want to arrange a meeting with a potential buyer. This means you must make a cold call to a complete stranger and convince him to give you some of his time. When you phone for an appointment, it must be done in a to-the-point manner. State your objective immediately; don't feel you have to start a relationship on the phone or fill him in on all the details surrounding your call. Just get his attention and save the details for your meeting. Here's an example:

"Hello, this is Joan Jones. Tom Johnson of Johnson Brothers tells me you are always on the lookout for a new, exciting product. He suggested I call you to arrange an appointment to show you the unique photo album I'm manufacturing that's been selling like hotcakes in all our local stores. Would Tuesday, March ninth at 10 AM be good for you?"

You have identified yourself, the purpose of your call and supplied a reference to inform the prospect that you have the credibility of pre-approval by someone he knows. If the product interests him and he respects the person who recommended you, he will agree to see you.

That's the professional way. Let me give you an example of how the inexperienced amateur would probably handle it, thereby immediately branding herself as a total unprofessional who would probably only waste his time.

"Hello, this is Joan Jones. I went to a wedding just last week and I met a man there named Tom Johnson. Well, we got to talking and I told him I just started a business making a new kind of photo album. I gave it to everyone for Christmas last year and they loved it. He told me he had just met you at the NOPA Show in Chicago—you had the booth next to his. He said you went out for a drink together and you mentioned that your company is always looking for new items. I live about forty miles from the city so I don't get in that often, but I thought I'd make a trip in next week and see as many people as I can in one day, and maybe I can come up to see you and show you my little album."

If the man is polite and not rushed at that moment, chances are he will listen to her patiently. But he will recognize that she is an amateur, the kind of inexperienced naif who can be a real pain to deal with since she will be unfamiliar with the industry and have to be led around by the nose. To a busy businessman, that is usually a big turn-off.

Your phone manner labels you a professional when you use the instrument for *communication, not conversation.* Explain who you are and how you came to call him. Naming a person with whom he is familiar conveys assurance that he will not be wasting his time and that you have something important to offer that might prove of value to him. If he wishes to question you further, fine. But let him do it, not you. When I advise that you speak in a direct businesslike manner, I don't mean that you should sound brusque and bloodless. Let your personality shine through and be friendly, but not familiar. Whenever I get a call that begins "May I speak to Cynthia Smith?" to which I respond "You are . . ." and the caller then says with phony geniality "Hello, Ms. Smith [or worse, Hi, Cindy], how are you today?" I know he's trying to sell me mutual funds or a cemetery plot and I end the call immediately.

Should you have to break or change an appointment, don't burden the listener with lengthy reasons. There's no need to feel guilty if you have to alter arrangements. Going into longwinded explanations borders on condescension; it implies you are so important to him that you feel you must ease the disappointment and pain of your postponement. Chances are he doesn't give a damn and doesn't feel that your visit will change his life any. Actually, it may not even be necessary to talk to him directly about a changed appointment; if he has a secretary, you can possibly set up the change with her since she probably keeps his schedule.

And while we're on the subject of proper telephone technique, let me warn you to keep the kids off the business phone. This is a hazard when you work at home and your children roam in and out of your office. A customer might get a kick out of it the first time your toddler picks up the phone and, when asked if his mother is home, answers yes and hangs up. The second time, when he needs a quick answer on a delivery date, might not be so amusing. The production manager of the company for which I was advertising director still laughs when he remembers my six-year-old picking up the phone and telling him I was unavailable because I was outside chasing her escaped pet rabbit. But I had been with the company for thirteen years and they were willing to accept the eccentricities of a working mother.

Positive Posture

Walk in like a wimp and you'll never walk out with the order. Yes, you're unsure. You've never tried selling yourself or your own creation to a tough businessman before. Slightly awed, you tend to be tentative about your presentation, uncertain of its value, and as a result, thoroughly unconvincing.

Let's start out with the awe. Who is this guy anyway?

Haven't you ever met a businessman before? That schlemiel living next door who always seems to be tripping over his lawn mower, your friend's motor-mouth husband whom everybody finds unbearable—they are businessmen. Do you think they are entitled to be treated with reverence just because they're seated behind a desk?

Consider yourself the equal of everyone you meet. If you have a bona fide product or service, then you're offering a resource for profit and benefit for *them*. They need you as much as you need them and you have no reason to feel subordinate: you have every right to be assertive and positive. You believe in the value of your offering and you should convey that belief strongly.

Now about that insecurity about your ability to sell. What do you mean you're inexperienced? Have you never raised funds for the PTA, your church or synagogue, or any charity? Have you never made calls to persuade voters to support your candidate? Have you never participated in a bake sale? And how about the selling job you had to do on your husband to get him to see the great benefits to be enjoyed from spending $5,000 on a Jacuzzi? Do not overlook the impassioned plea you made to your political science professor in college to get her to change your final grade from C to B.

The fact is, you've been selling all your life. You have the ability and the experience; all it takes is knowing your goals, your product, and your prospect. But it is imperative you come across as assured so that the person to whom you are making the pitch trusts your capability to successfully deliver whatever you promise.

Let me give you the key word to successful selling: self-benefit. Everyone you work with is looking to derive personal advantage from every negotiation. If your assertive posture convinces the listener that he will in any way benefit from the deal, be it commendation from his boss or profit for himself, you will get the sale.

How to Be a Boss

"You can become a friend of an employee, but never employ a friend."

This is an old business adage that I unfortunately had never heard of some years ago, when I made the error of asking a friend to work for me part-time. We arrived at an amicable per-hour figure but never discussed working conditions. The problem became apparent at lunchtime. My secretary, who had been with me for years, took out the lunch she had brought from home, filled her coffee mug from our always-on Bunnomatic, and proceeded to eat at her desk. My friend, however, looked at me expectantly. Since we had been serving each other food for years, she apparently never thought to bring a sandwich to my home. It dawned on me that she fully expected me to prepare and serve her lunch!

I disabused her of that notion fast by taking one container of yogurt out of the fridge and eating it at my desk while working. My secretary, who watched this little byplay with quiet amusement, directed my friend to a local take-out sandwich shop. She came back forty-five minutes later, reporting that she had gotten lost finding the place and the line had been long, then took another half-hour eating her lunch.

The following day, she announced that she had been so rushed that morning that she forgot to prepare any lunch, so it was back to the sandwich shop again and another hour-and-a-half lunch. (Remember she was getting paid by the hour.) The day after that, she came in with a large bag and announced triumphantly that she had brought lunch. Great. At twelve, she walked into my kitchen and asked for a frying pan and butter. She had brought two eggs and a basket of mushrooms, and she proceeded to make herself a mushroom omelet. The next time she came with eggs and a package of bacon. My secretary, who never took more than fifteen minutes for lunch, had a hard time keeping a straight face. I, who rarely even stopped for lunch, had a hard time keeping my temper.

How could I tell an old friend, who had always worked for large corporations, that she should have the sense to realize we are not General Motors and she's getting paid by the hour? How could I have known that she would be unable to distinguish between social and business relationships? The situation ended badly and damaged a friendship of many years. It's not always easy being the boss. Primarily, you must establish a position with your employees that clearly marks your authority; all other facets of the relationship are up to you.

Styles of management differ according to personalities. In a small business, where you all work together in close quarters, it's hard to be sharply authoritarian. You should be friendly, but clearly in charge. If you allow employees to become too familiar, you may find it hard to criticize their performance. And when you tell them to make certain corrections in their work, you may get an argument rather than acquiescence; you must let them know that you will listen to their opinions, but the final decision is yours alone.

Many neophyte employers mistakenly feel that the only way to establish authority is to act like tyrannical tycoons—barking instructions, bawling out workers, criticizing but never complimenting—the "let'em know who's boss" mode of management. This sort of treatment only antagonizes the staff and makes them unwilling to do more than minimally acceptable work.

I have had many employees, and have always found that it pays to be nice. Putting it in the crassest of terms, your object as a boss is to get the best possible performance and the most work out of your staff. Most people want to have the satisfaction of feeling they have accomplished their tasks well and that their work is appreciated. Give them clear instructions about what you expect and praise when it's done correctly, and they will bend over backward to produce for you. When errors are made, as will inevitably occur, first be sure that your instructions were absolutely clear; do not assume the worker is in the wrong until you know all the circumstances. There's nothing more embarrassing than a boss who berates and screams only to discover the employee was not at fault. Even if the worker was wrong, correct and explain patiently. I find that getting angry with an employee who has made a mistake, even when it's a really dumb mistake, is of no benefit to anyone and is in fact counterproductive. The employee gets so rattled that she's unable to work properly for hours. And in a small office, everyone hears the yelling and gets upset. The entire place is disrupted.

My first job was in a small advertising agency where we all worked in one big room. The owner was an erratic man who threw raging tantrums when things were not done to his liking. As a result, instead of trying to be innovative and turn out creative work—the aim of an advertising agency—we stuck to the old and hackneyed rather than risk his biting criticism and rejection. And nobody stayed a minute past five, even if we were in the middle of a job, because we hated the guy's guts and would not give him a shred more than the minimum.

I believe in the honor system: Put total trust in your employees. Everyone should know what her job entails, and should be trusted with the responsibility to fulfill her duties. If you respect her judgment, you will have no clock-watchers, and your office will have the general air of enthusiasm that makes for a pleasanter, more productive workplace. However, you must evolve your own style of management—one that you are comfortable with and that you find works well for you.

4

Your Business Blueprint: Checklist of Feasibility Factors

Starting a business is like building a house: before you start, you need a feasibility study to prove that the structure will be viable, and a blueprint to lay out details of exactly what will go where.

Preparing this "business blueprint" will help you face the realities you must deal with in your chosen business, and will validate your own faith in the project. It will also perform the important job of amassing the facts you will need for the business plan you must provide to banks or potential investors in order to get financing. What you must prove in your business plan is that there is a real need for your product or service and that you are ready and able to deliver it to the right market. (Instructions on how to prepare a business plan appear in chapter 6.) To help you work up your business blueprint, I have created what I call the "Feasibility Factor Checklist," which outlines the elements involved in building your kind of business. It gives you the questions you must ask yourself and others before you proceed with your venture.

FEASIBILITY FACTOR CHECKLIST

You Plan to Start a Retail Business

1. Is there a real long-term need for this type of business?

Just because you couldn't find the kind of apron you wanted last month does not necessarily justify your opening an apron store. You may love ceramic owls, but is the world ready for an owl shop? Don't permit your personal tastes and preferences to influence your judgment.

2. Have you picked the right neighborhood?

A designer clothes boutique or a caviar shop in a working-class area is usually not the best idea; however, there may be mitigating factors that would make this a good choice. One such factor is that the location borders on wealthier communities. For example, Port Chester, New York, is a blue-collar town with a depressed downtown that has become the home of a spate of upscale restaurants. This location is profitable because (1) Port Chester is abutted by and draws patronage from Rye, New York, and Greenwich, Connecticut, two of the richest towns in the East; (2) rents are cheap, which allows the restaurants to reap a greater profit margin; and (3) parking is plentiful and free.

3. Is this a suitably related environment?

If you are selling antiques, it is a good idea to be near other antique stores. Antique buyers do not shop for necessities; they are usually browsing for whatever catches their fancy, and they like to go from store to store. If you isolate yourself, you had better be certain that your wares are distinctive enough to induce collectors to make a special trip to reach you. Remember that you will be missing out on the overflow from other related shops.

The same applies to many other types of merchandise. Discount clothing stores usually group together to attract bargain-hunting buyers. You might find a cut-price shoe store adjacent to a cut-price handbag store, which is next door to a cut-price dress shop. That makes good sense.

In short, always seek a *related environment* that will insure the right traffic. You know your customer—look to place yourself near other stores that will regularly attract her or him. An athletic footwear store would do well next to a sporting goods equipment shop. Since fitness-conscious people are usually aware of their diets, a nearby health food store would also pick up patronage. It's a much faster road to success when you don't have to depend solely on advertising and word-of-mouth to build up clientele.

4.   Is it a convenient location?

There is a store in my town that I call The Revolving Door Store: it has the biggest turnover of proprietorships and must have the world's record of in-and-out owners. It's easy to see why retailers are drawn to it; it's on one of the busiest traffic streets in town and hundreds of cars pass by daily. Note the critical words "cars pass by": they *have* to because there's no place to park within a five-block radius. Unless you're locating on a city main street that gets primarily foot traffic, be sure there is accessible parking.

Look for a location that suits your goals. I had a student in my "How to Start a Business" course who told the class she planned to open a coffee shop next to a busy commuter railroad station, where she was counting on big morning rush-hour coffee-and-danish sales—both eat in and take-out. She told us she had already found a perfect location. I asked on which side of the train station she would be positioned; she said the north side. "But that's the coming-home side," I pointed out. "If you're selling breakfast, you have to be on the south going-to-work side." She literally turned pale. Luckily, the lease had not been finalized.

Often when you are excited by an idea and involved in a complicated negotiation, the simplest point is overlooked. Take your time and examine every situation carefully. Remember the classic byword in retailing: The three most important factors are location, location, and location.

5.   *If it's a mall, is it a good mall?*

I once did advertising and PR for a store located in a small shopping center—the kind of assemblage of anywhere from three to ten stores that is known in the industry as a "strip mall." My husband named it "dead center" because there was never anyone there. When I asked my client whatever possessed him to choose this particular center, his answer was, "It's in a nice community, it's on a busy thoroughfare, and the rent is reasonable." All true. It was a nice community and the mall was on a very heavily traversed main road but unfortunately, it was set so far back from that road and elevated so high above it that the stores were not visible. Secondly, the traffic pattern at that point was convoluted, which made entry and exit treacherous.

How could prospective tenants not realize that this is a loser location? All they had to do was check the number of cars parked in the lot. If you see ten cars parked in the lot at all times of day, shouldn't that tell you something? Especially when there are ten stores in the mall, which means the vehicles belong to store owners, not patrons. Check the parking lot for a few days; see how much traffic there actually is.

Another test of the value of a mall location is the store turnover. Before you sign the lease, find out how many of the stores have changed ownership in the past two years. And don't take the rental agent's word; go in and talk to the current store owners. Find out how much business they're doing before you plunge into placing your operation there.

You Plan to Start a Manufacturing Business

1.   Is there a realistic need for this product?

The bankruptcy rolls are filled with companies that manufactured items for which there was no demand. Most of those disasters could have been averted had someone made the effort and taken the time to do market research before jumping into production. No large company puts out a new product without first ascertaining that there is a viable market—enough people out there who will plunk down money for it to make the project profitable. So must you. Before going ahead with your plans to produce an item, first find out if anyone wants it. Just because you love the idea, and you think every home should have one, doesn't mean that the public shares your vision. True, it might be a handy item, but is it important enough to interest buyers?

Since I have been in the advertising and sales promotion business forever, people frequently approach me with ideas for products, which often puts me in the uncomfortable position of having to burst their bubble by explaining how their brother-in-law's opinion that it's a brilliant idea does not constitute grounds for go-ahead. One woman wanted to create an elegant silver holder for ketchup bottles until I pointed out that families who put condiment bottles on the table do not usually dine in a style that calls for twenty-five dollar ketchup covers. Another wannabe manufacturer came to me filled with wild enthusiasm for jazzy, decorative holders for Häagen-Dazs ice cream cartons. I gave her the ketchup-bottle analogy in reverse: people who buy expensive "boutique" ice cream would never commit the gaucherie of setting out ice cream containers at their dinner parties, and when it's for family eating, who needs fancy? Someone else was sure that men would go mad for a latherless shaving soap made in a tiny shop near the Brooklyn Bridge by an elderly man who claimed it was a "secret family formula" brought over from his native Hungary. I pointed out that many years ago when the major soap companies first introduced detergents (which actually create no suds), they were forced to put in sudsing elements because they found women connected suds to cleaning action. If you use soap, you want to see lather; otherwise how do you know it's doing anything?

2.   How will you produce the finished product?

Note the word "finished": that means fully packaged and ready for delivery. There are various alternatives here, and you must work them out in advance. Keep in mind that the more you can do yourself, in-house, the smaller your risk and start-up investment and the bigger your profit margin.

Produce it totally yourself: If it's a food, then you should start in your own kitchen, providing you can turn out enough to fill your starting orders. This is a practical, risk-free way to test the validity of your business; many a food empire was started in this fashion. You can always hire part-time or full-time help as sales increase, and when it gets to the point where you've outgrown the kitchen and the future looks promising, then you can take on the expense of moving to an outside facility. This same sort of do-it-all-yourself procedure can apply in other areas; hand-knit sweaters, for instance. Initially you will sell only your own output and when demand increases, you can farm out work to local knitters in a "cottage industry" method. Don't forget warehousing. Do you have space to store supplies and finished merchandise? Is there room in the garage or basement for inventory?

Produce it partially yourself: Outside contractors can supply the parts and you handle the assembly and packaging. Nina Webb, a Connecticut woman who designed a device to measure the height of tennis and racquetball nets, bought the brass chain and weights and hired people to sit in her basement assembling and packaging. Becky Mark, who created Cosmepak (a lucite holder for makeup), contracted out the manufacture of her product and handled the packaging and shipping in her basement. She had a large house and had plenty of room to store supplies, cartons, and products. Nina Webb's item was smaller; she stored finished merchandise under the dining room table.

Have the product totally produced for you: You may live in a three-room apartment and be unable to assume any of the tasks involved in the production of your items. Then you must find suppliers who will do the manufacturing, packing, warehousing, and shipping for you.

3.   How do you find suppliers?

Let your fingers do the walking—use the Yellow Pages. Another resource is the trade magazines of the industry you plan to enter; every field has a number of such publications. To find the ones you need, go to the reference room of your local library and ask for the *Standard Rate & Data Directories*. These are the media bibles that list every publication in the country; ask for the *Trade Magazine Directory* (with the green cover). Look for your industry (i.e., Food Service, Plastics) under the alphabetical categories and you will find the names, addresses, phone numbers, and names of staff members of all pertinent publications. Call, write, or fax the publisher or advertising manager of the magazine, and explain that you're a new manufacturer who is seeking suppliers and would like copies of the magazines and their recommendations. Note that I specified you contact the publisher or advertising manager. Since they recognize you as a potential source of income for them, they will want to help you grow to the point where you will place advertising in their publication. Actually, it's a good idea to read your trade magazines; not only will you get a feel and sense of the field but you will also learn about competitors, and important buying and selling trends.

Dealing with suppliers to get the best terms: Remember the firm stand you took with the plumber that made him bring his bill down from $300 to $225? And how you convinced the carpet cleaning company to do your bedroom free because you argued that it came under the total square footage that was in their printed offer? That's negotiating, and that's what you must do when you deal with suppliers from whom you will be buying goods and services. It's no different than what you have been doing. Don't be awed because you're sitting in his office rather than your home—money is money and business is business, no matter where it's transacted. It's merely a matter of each side trying to make the best possible deal for him or herself.

Act professional and to the point. Be specific in what you want him to do. Prepare your questions beforehand; lay out your needs, specifications, and goals. Don't paint an unrealistic pie-in-the-sky picture about expecting to sell millions; he knows a first order can lead to bigger orders, but businessmen must deal with Now. Don't be vague; specify quantities expected, delivery dates, and details of payment. He will probably demand COD (cash on delivery) until you have established your credit reliability. Ask for quantity discounts and the price break points: the 1–100 price is $4.50 each and you may want 100. But the 101–200 price is $4.25. You'll never know unless you ask questions. Who are their other customers so that you can call them for references? Do they have the equipment and facilities to fulfill your needs and the scheduling capability to assure on-time deliveries? These kinds of questions will earn his respect, so that he doesn't look upon you as a naive housewife he can take advantage of; be firm but don't put on a tough-guy act because you think that's good business. Negotiating is the art of getting what you want, and that means you have to understand his business and needs as well as yours so that both you and he will benefit from the arrangement.

4.   How will you sell your product?

OK, you've turned out a great product. Now how do you get it to market? How do you reach the buyers?

There are a number of options, but *you* are the prime doer.

Going store to store yourself: Load up your car and go from store to store to peddle your wares: it's as simple as that. Retailers will see you because they are out to sell goods, and if you have an item that will move and produce profit, they'll be interested. Actually, you are the best salesperson for your merchandise because you believe in it, and nothing is more convincing than the enthusiasm of a true believer. However, be realistic. Don't be dejected if not every store buys, and don't expect the ones that do to place big starting orders. Put yourself in their shoes: would you be willing to put out big bucks for an untried product? The way to induce them to buy is by offering to take back unsold merchandise after a sensible period. Who could resist such a risk-free opportunity?

Circularizing stores (direct mail):   Send a letter, with a brochure or circular, to stores throughout the country. This doesn't preclude your going from store to store but allows you to reach faraway potential customers, and also introduces you to ones you do eventually visit.

Setting up a sales organization: There's only so much ground that you can physically cover, and so many places you can be. Once sales have reached a fair level, it will be time to pass the task of selling on to other hands.

You now have two choices: Distributors and/or manufacturers' representatives. A distributor is a company with a warehouse where they store large supplies of merchandise purchased from manufacturers like you, which they then resell to stores. Manufacturers' reps are merely sales agents for you: they sell your stuff to stores, you ship to and bill each store and send a monthly sales commission to the rep. Both distributors and reps operate within a specific industry; for example, an office supplies distributor or rep will carry lines of merchandise only for that industry and will make calls only on office supply stores.

Once you have established a track record that shows there's a viable market for your product, you can seek out distributors and/or reps to handle your products. They operate geographically, which means you will need one for the East Coast, another for the West Coast, and so on.

Good ones are very choosy and it is quite a victory to have your line taken on by a major rep or distributor. To find out who's who, call the trade magazines of your industry; they have lists of all distributors and manufacturers' reps in the field and will frequently be happy to recommend suitable organizations. They can be a great help, because the publisher and advertising manager must keep their ears to the ground in the field to be effective; they know who's selling what to whom, and often know which rep has just lost a line and is looking for new ones.

You Plan to Start a Mail-Order Business

Mail order, now known as "direct response," means selling directly to the end user. No salespeople, no stores—the entire transaction, from purchase to receipt of merchandise, is accomplished entirely by mail. There are two ways you can go into the mail-order business: (1) set up your own company and handle everything from advertising to shipping, or (2) sell products to a mail-order catalog company that does it all for you.

Establishing Your Own Mail-Order Company

This requires the big up-front expense of buying advertising space in magazines, or sending out your own mailing. Just to give you some idea of how big the cash outlay can be, the minimum size ad (1/12th page—2-1/4 × 2-1/2″) in *House Beautiful*'s shopping section costs $2,665. Can you imagine how many widgets you have to sell to cover the cost of the ad, let alone to generate profit?

If you decide to take this direct response route, here are a few smart-buying tips that will mark you as a pro. If you contract for a few ads with any of the magazines' shopping sections, ask for a deal to give you a proportionate number of free editorials, which are often as or more effective than actual ads. And speaking of deals, today's savvy media buyer knows that, unlike years ago when the space prices quoted in their rate cards were sacrosanct, magazines will negotiate. In fact, *House Beautiful* or any of the other publications with mail-order sections are often willing to go as low as fifteen percent off the rate card cost. Just *ask*.

Many successful businesses have started via the direct response route. For one thing, it enables you to find out quickly if there is a market for your product. For instance, if you run an ad for your widget and get five responses, it might be time to reconsider the enterprise. However, should you draw a slew of orders, you not only have proven the desirability of your product to you but to stores that might now be willing to stock it. Some business starters have taken the personal gamble of running an ad before going for financing, and then walking into the bank with a bag full of ad responses to prove the desirability of their products. Becky Mark launched her Cosmepak with an ad in the *New York Times* mail-order section; her products are now sold in department and drug stores throughout the country.

A mail-order business always seems attractive to starter-uppers. It sounds easy and fun: you run an ad and just sit back and wait for the money to pour in. That's true—if you never plan to make it big. In actuality, the mail-order business has become highly computerized, cutthroat, and costly. In order to grow, you will have to develop a mailing list of customers to whom you will periodically send out expensive-to-produce-and-mail catalogs, which means that you will need to expand your product line—beyond your original product—in order to make a profit. All this is feasible, especially if you specialize in a specific category of product and customer. Let's say you have an item for mountain climbers and backpackers. You could expand your line to include other products of interest to this market and print up a simple one-color catalog. (This is a purist group who expect simplicity and are actually turned off by glitzy four-color, shiny paper booklets that are not biodegradable.)

You Plan to Start a Business Selling Products to Mail-Order Companies

This is truly the easy way. You merely deliver your product to a mail-order company, who then features it in their catalog—no busting your butt selling store to store; no packing, shipping, and mailing one at a time; no big up-front advertising costs. You just make a mass quantity shipment to one source, and they sell thousands and send you a check. Sounds great, right? But of course, it's a bit more complicated than that.

Dealing with mail-order catalog companies

First, find all the mail-order catalogs that carry the type of merchandise you produce and make your pitch to them. According to Edith Goldman, catalog manager for Hanover Direct (one of the largest mail-order companies in the world), it is imperative that you "determine the mission of the particular catalog, who is the customer they are trying to sell. Remember that every catalog is targeted to a specific kind of person. If your product fits the needs of that individual, it has a chance of getting into the catalog. We're always looking for interesting or different items, or items that fill a niche."

That would mean Nina Webb's tennis net measurer would be suitable for sporting goods catalogs. If you had designed a special neck pillow, which is always in demand since neckaches are one of the most prevalent health problems today, you would direct your item to bed-and-bath catalogs.

Your next step is sending sales information to the buyers for these catalogs. Your mailing should include a photo and description of your product, pricing details, and a letter explaining why the product is good, unique, different, and why it will sell to that catalog's customers. Don't assume that the benefits of your product are self-evident and that the buyer will instantly recognize why people will desire your item; she's not that perceptive. Include an offer to send a sample "on memo." That term means it's not free, and you will bill her within thirty days if she doesn't return the item. Of course, if you get a big order, you don't charge for the sample and if your item is priced under ten dollars, you'll probably never see it again. But the "on memo" stipulation puts her on notice not to toss the item out or just give it to the receptionist.

Now comes the tough part—quantity. When you deal with catalog companies, remember that they mail to millions and you have to be prepared to fill whatever orders are generated. According to Ms. Goldman, "We usually place a minimum order of at least three hundred with a guarantee that the vendor can turn out another large quantity within three weeks."

By law, mail-order companies must fill an order within thirty days of receipt of the order or go through the added expense of advising the customer of delay. Since they cannot initially predict how many orders will come in, they must be certain you can produce sizable quantities quickly if the item takes off. If they are forced to accumulate sizable back orders because you are unable to deliver merchandise as needed, that first order may be your last.

Some buyers may ask that you guarantee to have two or three thousand on hand for instant backup. They can ask, but you don't have to do it; the number is negotiable. If you can't be sure of disposing of that many pieces elsewhere should the buyer decide not to take them, you could be stuck with a big inventory. Be realistic, and don't allow the buyer to push you into a potentially money-losing proposition. You can say "no" and still not jeopardize the order. You can sell to as many catalog companies as possible; exclusivity is not demanded. If your item pulls, you can develop a nice steady business, but you cannot depend on a constant level of buying interest forever, which is why you must diversify. A one-item mail-order business will rarely make you rich.

According to Frances Needles, marketing director of Hearst Magazines Direct Response Home Group: "Unfortunately, in mail order, there's no way to accurately predict which item will sell like a winner and which will fall flat on its face."

According to Ms. Needles, her department will help any potential entrepreneur get started. "Mail order is our business, and we're glad to offer whatever guidance we can."

Just write to:

Hearst Magazines Direct Response Home Group
224 West 57th Street
New York, New York 10019

There's a lot to be learned about the mail-order business and there are many books on the subject, but your best resource for current information on the industry is the trade organization:

Direct Marketing Association
6 East 43rd Street
New York, New York 10017–4646

You Plan to Start a Service Business

1.   Is there a realistic need for your service and are you qualified to deliver it?

Since women have become aware of the value of networking, local associations of women business owners have sprung up all over the country. Their published directories contain a wide spectrum of ideas for businesses—some showing intelligence and creativity and others demonstrating a poor grasp of the realities of the world of commerce. Each listing has a description of the enterprise, and some of them make you wonder about the kind of myopic conceit that makes anyone believe people would pay for services—usually described with vague flowery descriptions—like "My programs help you gain the success and self-fulfillment you want and deserve" (listed under "Business Consultants") or "Corporate image impact . . . dress for professional and business women and men" (listed under "Image Consultants"). There is no mention of what qualifies these women to perform these services, and one wonders for whom?

There are usually a large number of bookkeeping services for small businesses. In every area, there are hundreds of small businesses that do not have the volume of work to require a staff bookkeeper, or the time and ability to handle it themselves; they use a service to prepare payrolls, taxes, and other accounting work. If you are good with figures and have a comprehensive computer program to perform these tasks, this may be an excellent choice for a business.

The lovely part of starting a service business is that it requires almost no start-up outlay or investment other than printing cards, stationery, and brochures. The keys to starting a service business with a chance of growth and success are (1) it must offer a service for which there is a current and future market so that you can depend on repeat business rather than one-shot sales; and (2) you must be well-qualified to supply that service.

How to Price Your Product or Service

Two women in my University of Connecticut class started a small mail-order business selling lucite products for the home, and they asked me to prepare an ad for them for placement in *House Beautiful*'s shopping section. I photographed the item—a roll-around plant stand—and wrote suitable copy based on the information they gave me. When the ad appeared in the spring issue of the magazine, I was horrified to see someone else's ad on the facing page featuring the identical product for ten dollars less. When I called them to question their pricing, they said in perfect logic "We just figured what we paid for the item and added a markup." "But didn't you check the market to see how comparable items were priced?", I asked. They seemed stunned at the concept. "But if we charged any less, we wouldn't make any profit."

Needless to say, their business did not last long and neither, I might add, did their friendship.

Establishing proper pricing is critical in any business; many failures have been caused by incorrect calculations that led to mispricing. Whether it's a retail, manufacturing, or service business, cost and profit factors must be examined carefully.

It's not complicated; in fact, it's fairly simple. First, you must compute *all* your costs carefully, being sure to overlook nothing, including materials (equipment and supplies), wages and salaries, overhead (rent, utilities, maintenance), taxes, sales commissions, shipping, warehousing, insurance, advertising, returned merchandise, and unpaid debts. All of these factors have to be fed into the hopper to determine your cost of operation. You can then figure how much markup you must place on every item you buy or produce in order for you to cover costs and make a profit. The next step is to check the market for comparable products so that you can ascertain whether your selling prices will be within the parameters of the industry.

Now comes the final analysis. If you find that the prices you must charge in order to make a profit are far lower than prevailing prices, go back and refigure: you may have overlooked an important element. I once had a printer forget to include the cost of ink in his estimate; sometimes it's the simple, obvious things we forget. If it still comes out right, then you have two choices: charge the accepted going rates and reap big immediate profits, or come in lower and make a fair profit per unit but probably achieve a greater volume of sales and build up a big buying constituency. If your price must be higher than comparable merchandise or services in order for you to make a profit, then it's time again to go back and refigure. If you still find that you must charge more, examine the benefits your product offers compared to the others. Maybe yours is better, and if it is superior in ways that customers are willing to pay more for, then go for it.

Pomodoro Fresca Pasta Sauce is made of fresh tomatoes, olive oil, olives, basil, garlic, salt, and pepper; a 4-ounce serving contains 28 calories, 5 grams of carbohydrates, and 41 milligrams of sodium. It is sold in upscale supermarkets and gourmet food shops for about five dollars for a 16-oz. jar. Ordinary pasta sauces are usually made of ground tomatoes in puree, water, tomato paste, sugar, salt, soybean oil, dehydrated onions, lemon juice, parsley flakes, garlic, pepper, and spices; a 4-ounce serving is 90 calories, 12 grams of carbohydrates, and 725 milligrams of sodium. They are sold in supermarkets for about two dollars for a 16-oz. jar. The consumer who is concerned about nutrition, freshness of contents, calorie and sodium intake, and who has a more discerning palate, will be happy to pay more. Pomodoro Fresca is aiming for a different market than the ordinary pasta sauce and thus can ask for and get more.

Pricing is the way people determine the value of your product or service. If someone saw two seemingly identical glasses side-by-side in a store, one priced at three dollars and the other at five dollars, she would make an immediate assumption that the five-dollar one is in some way better, and if she wanted a finer glass, she would buy the higher-priced one. Remember that it is often difficult for buyers to discern differences in quality and they use the price tag to make the determination for them. I had a client who manufactured ice buckets and had to come out with a new design every year. One year, he designed a unit that consisted of an insulated metal container with Portuguese cork affixed on all five sides; the result was a stark, simple box. It was easy to assemble and the materials were inexpensive, so he priced the piece at $9.95 retail and shipped them out to all his customer stores, who ordered freely because they knew they had return privileges—of which they availed themselves liberally. The ice bucket bombed. He assumed the seasoned manufacturer's philosophy of "sometimes you win, sometimes you lose" and gave up on the item. Then, lo and behold, the Museum of Modern Art in New York City chose the stark, simple, form-following-function ice bucket as a winner of its prestigious design-of-the-year award, and my client realized he had been pitching to the wrong market. He changed the retail price to twenty-five dollars, sent it to his upscale stores, and the item sold out. The fact is that people who are in the market for a twenty-five-dollar ice bucket would not be interested in one bearing a mere $9.95 price tag.

The moral of the story? Don't be afraid to charge more if you have a distinctive product or service. The price you set enables the customer to instantly place a value on the product and positions it in the market.

5

How to Set Up Your Business: The Legal and Financial Facts of Life

OK, everything's in place for your business start-up. You know what to do, where and how you will do it. Now it's time to take official steps to put your plans into reality. Unfortunately, gone are those simple times when one could start an enterprise just by putting out a shingle and opening your doors; those days you were truly in business for yourself. Today you have a built-in mandatory partner (the Government) which means forms, taxes, and regulations—which means you need a lawyer and an accountant.

No problem, you think. "My neighbor is the controller of some big corporation downtown, I'll ask him to do me a favor and moonlight by handling my accounting. And my cousin Louie passed the bar last month. He'll work cheap."

Think again. There are big costs for such favors—being hesitant about bothering a friend or neighbor with questions, feeling ungracious about contesting his conclusions and recommendations, and being unable to insist upon on-time delivery of information and tax forms. Why should you put yourself in the hat-in-hand position of feeling beholden to someone who is actually working for and getting paid by you? Why should your work have to be done only when he can squeeze it into *his* schedule, which inevitably means missing dates for filing tax returns and asking the IRS for extensions? And then there is the major factor of his competence to handle small-business needs when his expertise and experience have only been in big business. He may be a honcho with hot-and-cold running secretaries, but would he be able to work out an assessment resolution with the state department of taxation for an $84.75 overcharge?

As for cousin Louie, you get what you pay for. He may have been first in his class in law school, and be a hotshot on torts and litigation, but what does he know about small business?

This is *serious business*, not some casual hobby. You need competent, professional practitioners who are experts in dealing with small businesses, who are familiar with all pertinent Federal and State regulations, and who understand the budget limitations of a minimally-financed company.

Look for a lawyer and accountant who are local and have small business clients. Friends, husbands, and relatives may suggest their "big downtown" attorneys and accountants and be condescending about small-town talents. But often these big-time firms won't take on small accounts and even if they would, they are used to handling million-dollar-deals, which means you will get short shrift and frequently mismanagement, procrastination, and postponement.

The lawyer will probably be a one-time deal; you may need her services only for forming your business. The same does not apply to your accountant, whose services will be required throughout the year at intervals determined by your needs.

When you're starting out, you or an associate or employee should be able to handle the bookkeeping with a computer (see chapter 9 on computers). If you do not feel ready for a computer or don't have the time to take care of accounts payable, accounts receivable, inventory, and other financial details, you may prefer to turn them over to a bookkeeping service. However, if your business is complicated and involves many elements, you may be best off doing minimal bookkeeping ledger maintenance yourself and using the services of an accountant on a monthly basis.

As explained by H. Cappy Riemer, a CPA at Bolnick, Snow and Riemer in Brewster, New York, "If you had a mail-order business that required shipping merchandise throughout the country, you would have to contend with different local sales taxes which you must charge each customer and then turn over to each government. To give you some idea of the extent of this complication, there are fifty to sixty different tax rates for different towns and municipalities in New York State alone."

There's another decision to be made about choosing an accountant—should you get an accountant or a CPA. Both may have had the same basic education and received degrees in accounting, but to reach a higher level, one must pass an examination that entitles him to put the letters CPA after his name, signifying he has achieved the professional distinction of Certified Public Accountant. In addition, CPAs, like doctors, must maintain specified continuing education requirements which guarantee that they keep abreast of the latest regulations.

Which Type of Business Ownership Is Best for You?

The most important thing to discuss with both your lawyer and accountant is the kind of formal structure you want for the business. As advised by Mr. Riemer, "You have a number of choices, and your accountant and lawyer will point out the particular advantages and drawbacks of each form as well as helping you decide which one fits your special situation."

Sole Proprietorship: It's your baby, yours and yours alone. Maybe you want to give it your name, like "Martha Jones Catering," or perhaps you want to call it by some special appellation like "Great Eating." All you have to do is go to your county offices and register with the County Clerk as "Martha Jones d/b/a Great Eating." (d/b/a stands for "Doing Business As.") Actually, you don't need a lawyer at all to set up this kind of business, but it's still a good idea to see him first to help you decide whether this is the best route for you to take.

Partnership: If two or more of you will work together to build this business you absolutely need a lawyer to protect each one's rights and clearly spell out proportions of financial interest and ownership, and to prepare for possible future contingencies, like death or defection of one partner. How much would your partner's share be worth? How would you be able to handle the payout? For this setup, you will need partnership insurance.

A partnership is often described as a marriage without love, so you can imagine the possible pitfalls. Everything may start out amicably, but you can't count on that lovey-dovey climate to last forever. It may well continue, but horror stories abound about partner differences. The power of money to destroy relationships is incredible. When business is good, everyone's happy and there are usually no problems. But when things get slow, which is inevitable, fear causes nerves to fray and tempers to rise. "Why did you order all those blue shirts we're stuck with?" "I told you we shouldn't extend so much credit to the Acme store. I said he was a deadbeat." The free-floating "Why didn't you's?" and "I told you so's" will cause friction and fury.

Then there is the competition between the "inside person" and the "outside person," which can eventually lead to hassles. In a manufacturing business, one partner usually handles the "inside" responsibilities like production and administration, and the other partner is the "outside" person who deals with sales. Each one is convinced she is mainly responsible for the success of the company. The "outside" partner feels she is the one who brings in the business, while the "inside" partner feels put upon because she's stuck in the plant dealing with the stress of running the place while her colleague is out there running around, wining and dining on company funds. Such fires are often fed by family members (usually spouses) who for some ulterior motive—I suspect pure jealousy—point out how much more one partner is doing than the other, so why should they both take home equal money? Many businesses have been destroyed by such internecine battles.

Another point of concern in partnerships is that each partner is held liable for the actions of the other. You may like your partner and have known her for years. You trust her honesty, but how about her judgment? You could be hung up for debts she incurred without your knowledge or approval. This is why, though technically you can start a partnership business in the same simple way as a sole proprietorship by merely registering with the Country Clerk, you had better talk to a lawyer first to protect yourself.

Corporation: When you start a business, you're filled with hope, enthusiasm, and the expectation of success. In olden times they used to kill the bearer of bad tidings, which is probably what you will feel like doing to your lawyer when he points out possible financial disasters and suggests ways to insulate you against them.

If your business could incur financial risks for which you would not like to be held personally responsible, then your lawyer or accountant will probably suggest you form a corporation. The corporation is regarded by the government as a separate entity (almost a person) and is taxed accordingly, but any liability that occurs in the business is borne by this faceless entity, which means you will not be held personally responsible. Say you sign a five-year lease for the business and things don't work out as planned, so you close your doors after two years. If you personally signed the lease, you will have to pay the rent for the remaining three years. If your business is a corporation and the corporation is defunct, the obligation is not yours and it's tough noogies for the landlord. Or say someone slips on the sidewalk in front of your store and sues for three million dollars. If you're a sole proprietorship, even assuming you're insured, you will have to pay any difference between the insurance company's obligation and the huge figure the claimant will probably be awarded. Personal injury, product liability—these can generate

huge liabilities for which you can be held personally responsible unless you are incorporated.

Should the business end for whatever reason, all contractual
obligations for goods and services are viewed as corporate and
you are off the hook. The only financial obligations for which
corporate officers are personally liable forever are those known
as fiduciary—sales, payroll, employment, and other taxes.

If you incorporate with other people, then you should protect
yourself against dissolution, dissension, or death. You will need
a shareholder's agreement to determine what happens to an individual's shares in the corporation should she leave for any reason. How would you like to be faced with the sudden tragic loss
of your co-owner, then find out you now have an unexpected
new business partner—the snotty MBA son who inherited her
shares?

Once you have decided that incorporating is the way to go,
you have to select which of two types of corporations you prefer:

> **C Corporation:** This is the common one. All the profits
> and losses accrue solely to the corporation. You can only
> take out money as salary.
>
> **S Corporation:** All the same limited liability benefits as
> the C corporation, but here you can withdraw money from
> the profits and take a personal tax deduction for any cor-
> porate losses. This last feature is attractive if you are for-
> tunate enough to have a private income or file a joint
> return with a husband who has a large income, in which
> case the corporate loss can be used as a deduction to
> reduce your personal taxes. Since most businesses show a
> loss the first year (at least), why not get some personal
> advantage? When the business becomes profitable, you
> can always elect to switch to a C corporation.

Now you can see why you *must* talk to a lawyer and an accountant before you begin operation. See a few before you decide on

the right one for you. Other than the fact that they must be experienced in small business, you may want to be sure they're on your wave length. At the risk of offending the Internal Revenue Service, let me point out that there are gray areas of interpretation of the tax laws. Barring any activity that constitutes fraud, which is plain foolish and wrong, accountants view deduction eligibility in different ways. You may feel more comfortable with the rigid stickler type, or prefer the more laissez-faire kind. It's important to like the professionals you work with because you have to trust them, and talk to them a good deal; it's so much pleasanter when you're compatible with them.

Don't forget to discuss fees up front. Some professionals charge on a straight fee-for-the-job basis; there is usually a fixed price for setting up a corporation, which varies tremendously from town to town. Some charge an hourly rate. Some want monthly retainers, depending on the nature of the work expected. Whatever arrangement you make, be sure you do it at the outset so there are no surprises.

Taxes: A Serious Fact of Life

Let me give you a very important business maxim that could save you from a future of misery: *ALWAYS PAY YOUR TAXES ON TIME*. You can juggle all other bills, maybe put off a few invoices until next month, but *never delay paying the government*.

In a small business, especially a start-up, cash flow is a common problem. Customers don't always pay on time—some take sixty days to pay, some take ninety—but you know they're good for the money so you have little choice but to wait. The little guy, like you, always gets paid last. As a result, there will be times when you are strapped and unable to pay all your bills on time. Let's say among them is a bill for $3,000 from the federal government for withholding tax.

There are various state and federal taxes that are required of every business and payments are usually due quarterly and annually. When you have employees, you must withhold portions of their wages which you then turn over to the government. When you charge sales tax, you must pay that to the state government, usually quarterly. In business, you act as a collecting agent for the government; it's actually *their* money and must be paid to them on schedule.

At bill-paying time, you sit at your desk looking at the pile of invoices: who to pay and who to delay? Decisions will, of course, be based on the importance of each creditor to your business. You owe your major supplier $3,000; you depend on him to provide the materials that keep your business going and can't afford to antagonize him, so you decide to use the $3,000 you had allocated for taxes to pay the supplier. You figure that maintaining a credit rating with him is more critical to the day-by-day operation of your business than is your credit status with the government. Besides, the government doesn't hound you with embarrassing, annoying bill-collector calls like private creditors. They don't have to: they know they'll always get theirs, no matter what. So you say to yourself: "No problem, I'll just double up on my next quarterly tax payment."

Next quarter comes around and this time you need $6,000. How can you possibly take that much cash out of the business? So you let it slip until the next quarter, and soon you have what has become a crippling debt *that you personally can never escape*. Even if your corporation should fail and go out of business, even if you file for bankruptcy: *THE OFFICERS OF THE CORPORATION ARE PERSONALLY RESPONSIBLE FOR REPAYING ALL OBLIGATIONS TO THE GOVERNMENT . . .* forever.

I know a man who had a small store that sold mattresses. He made the mistake of holding back state sales tax payments and using the money for other business needs. After a few years the store went under and he filed for bankruptcy, which protected him against claims from all creditors—except the government. He had amassed such a huge unpaid tax debt that today—ten years later—he is still unable to get back on his feet. The government will take any money he earns until they collect the entire amount he owes, which grows constantly since the interest accrues daily. He also finds it difficult to get a job because employers do not want the bookkeeping bother of garnisheeing a salary, which means taking special deductions and sending the amount to the government. He cannot own anything because the government has the right to put a lien on (take possession of) any asset he has.

You may be the kind of conscientious person who prides herself on paying bills on time and who enjoys excellent credit everywhere. Going into business may force you to change these habits and bend the rules a bit. Small businesses are chronically underfinanced and keeping a balance between accounts payable and accounts receivable is not always possible. Don't get upset if you have to pay some bills in sixty days or more. Once they know you're dependable and will pay eventually, debtors will adjust their schedules. In the current business climate, everyone is used to delayed payments and will usually go along with you.

One likes to think only about potential success when starting any endeavor. That's as it should be. But always be aware of the possible downside, as well as the upside, so that you are prepared. Filing for bankruptcy would relieve the corporation and you of the burden and obligation of repaying all business debts, *except to the government* to whom you remain personally liable forever.

6

Finding Financing: How Much Money You Need and Where to Get It

Going to Banks for Backing

Whenever I see that great movie classic *It's a Wonderful Life*, shown on TV almost daily over the Christmas holidays, I get teary with nostalgia, especially when I see James Stewart giving loans to townspeople just for the asking. Gone are those warm and friendly days when you could walk into your local bank and get money virtually on a handshake. When I started my advertising agency twenty-five years ago, I was granted a $5,000 business loan based merely on the fact that I am a homeowner and had an excellent credit record. Today, banking regulations have become restrictive and bankers are no longer able or willing to extend credit based on the fact that they know you have a sterling character, superb credit record, and are a pillar of the community. They demand collateral of some sort to secure the loan.

Banks are no longer the solid, substantial source of financing they once were. Twenty-five years ago, you rarely heard of a bank failure. Today, after the S&L debacle, you hear more and more of banking institutions that are shaky. As a result, they are loathe to take the risks they once could afford, and start-up businesses are the riskiest of all. As one bank loan officer said to me: "We can read the past but not the future. We have no crystal balls, and with a start-up situation, there's no track record or history to guide us, no clue as to how the business will fare."

As a result, it is difficult, *but not impossible*, to get loans to finance a start-up business. As I learned, loan policies vary from bank to bank.

I called many different banks for facts on their lending specifications for beginner entrepreneurs and here are the answers I received:

1. "We *never* give loans to start-ups unless we get liquid collateral that we can convert to cash easily."
2. "We give loans for start-ups, but people have to come to us with a well-thought-out and planned package that looks good so that we can go to the SBA (Small Business Administration) and get them to guarantee it."
3. "We won't bother with small loans; it's not cost-efficient for us. Our minimum loan is $25,000."
4. "We'll lend as little as $2,500."

As you can see, different lenders have different policies on start-up financing, which means you should not take the word of one local bank as the gospel of the industry. Ask around, and don't confine yourself to one area: go to the nearest city or to neighboring communities and towns. Before you take the trip, however, call and ask the loan officer to explain the details of that bank's policy on start-up loans. *Shop for a bank the way you shop for a car ... go from bank to bank to find the best buy.*

Almost every bank will extend loan financing if you bring in suitable collateral. Collateral is some form of asset that can be converted to cash, like stocks, bonds, CDs, or the cash value of insurance policies. In other words, they will give you money only if you have money. I can hear you saying, "If I have the money, what do I need them for?" The difference is, you do not have to actually spend your money, or cash in bonds, stocks, or CDs. You hand over the assets for collateral, and the bank just holds them; that's their security to assure they will get their money should you default. Your assets continue to earn interest and dividends, and when the loan is repaid, everything is returned to you in tact. In other words, you get your assets to work for you.

If you don't have enough collateral, perhaps a family member or friend would be willing to pledge her securities for your loan. Given the fact that those securities are probably just sitting in a drawer or vault accumulating interest, nothing will change except that everything moves to your bank's vault. She must be told, of course, that should your business not work out and you are unable to repay the loan personally, she stands to lose her money. It is a risk, but if someone believes in your venture and trusts your honor, she could be willing to help.

If you own a home, you can take out a home equity loan where the bank lends you money based on the value of your home, or you can take out a second mortgage.

Other Sources of Financing: Outside Investors

It is often possible to interest a friend or relative in coming in with you as a more-or-less silent partner. If it looks like an enterprise that can produce far more for them than the small percentage of interest their money is earning from CDs and money market accounts, many people are willing to take such risks.

The young man who started the Subway hero sandwich business got his start with an investment from a man who asked for fifty percent of the profits in return for his $10,000 start-up capital. The business grew into one of the country's major franchise operations and that investor is now rolling in wealth. When you are looking for what is known as venture capital, you must be prepared to give away at least fifty percent of the business. Don't be indignant and resistant to the idea, even though it sounds terrible at first: "It's my brainchild, I'll be doing all the work and giving it all my time and life. And you want half?" Relax and remember, half of something is better than all of nothing.

The All-Important Business Plan

Why you need a business plan

You may think you are a dynamite communicator and can make a persuasive pitch for financing your project. That's wonderful, as long as you back it up with facts, figures, and documentation. No bank or sophisticated investor will give you a dime unless they are certain you know what you're doing, have a fairly good chance of success, and that their money will be secure.

They want to see a carefully substantiated business plan that not only provides information to prove the potential profitability of your project, but also demonstrates your business sophistication and capability to carry the whole thing off.

How to prepare your business plan

First, make a checklist of the realistic financial needs of your type of business. The key word here is "realistic." Exactly how much money will be required to get your business up and running? The beginner's tendency is to downplay her start-up fiscal needs on the assumption that it's easier to get a smaller business loan than a big one. Wrong! Undercapitalization is the major cause of new business failures, and banks and investors will have no faith in an entrepreneur who underestimates her financial projections. Also keep in mind that institutions and individuals who extend loans seek profit and security for their money, and would rather give large loans to substantial companies than small loans to untried projects with questionable futures. It's not how much you ask for that matters so much as how well you substantiate your demands, thereby assuring the loaner of your capability to repay the loan with interest.

When you work out your realistic fiscal requirements, there are two areas of need to be considered: the Business and You. Let's begin with the Business.

Retailing

Before you open your doors, you'll have some major one-time expenses.

Pre-Opening Costs: Fixtures, furniture, bags and boxes, stationery (business cards, invoices), decor both interior and exterior. (Special tip: Before you get involved with signs or an awning, check with local building regulations. Many towns have regulations about the size and style of store exteriors. If you have an eating place, you may want to set up some outdoor tables. Check the rules.) And then there's stock; you must have a full, extensive line of merchandise for your grand opening because that's your one chance to present to prospective customers the character of your store and the promise of what they can expect from you.

Constant Monthly Costs: Rent, restocking merchandise, employee salaries, cleaning, insurance, utilities, bookkeeping and accounting, delivery service, advertising.

My Uncle Al, a pharmacist, was a terrible businessman. My father, a superb businessman, would get aggravated every time he visited his brother's drugstore and watched customers come in for specific drug products that Uncle Al did not have in stock.

"I'll order it for you" was his inevitable answer. As the customer walked out, undoubtedly heading for the nearest competitive pharmacy, my father would fume and ask why he never seemed to have anything on hand other than aspirin.

"But if I stock too much and no one comes in to buy it, I'll be stuck with a big inventory," argued Uncle Al.

"If you keep this up, soon no one will come in to buy anything," said my father. "If people can't depend on finding what they want here when they need it, they'll develop the habit of going elsewhere. Then you won't have to worry about too much inventory because you won't have any business."

My father was right. Uncle Al's policy was a self-fulfilling prophecy and he eventually did go bankrupt.

There's nothing more deadly than a store with sparse stock, or one that continues to feature the same merchandise because business is slow and the owner is afraid to invest in new inventory. Customers who come in for a specific item leave in disappointment; customers who come in to browse and see the same merchandise week after week lose interest and never return. That's why you must figure constant inventory development into your costs.

Manufacturing

Pre-Opening Costs: Equipment, furniture, raw materials, packaging materials.

Constant Monthly Costs.   Rent (unless you plan to operate from home), restocking materials, employee wages, cleaning, insurance, utilities, legal, bookkeeping and accounting, delivery service, advertising.

Service

The best part of a service business, and why so many people go into one, is that start-up costs and constant monthly costs are minimal. All you need is stationery, business cards, and a telephone. Bookkeeping and accounting are usually fairly simple since you don't have many different types of expenses. Advertising in publications and sending out mailings would be about it.

Now that you have all the start-up and constant expenses, total them up. Start-up is a one-time cost, but monthly expenses can go on for as long as it takes for the business to go into profit, which could be two years. You have to have enough money to cover expenses for as long as it takes for the business to generate income, so when you are working up these numbers, figure in the amounts you need to keep production and sales moving until accounts receivable come in.

Once you have computed all your expenses, you know what it will cost to get the business started and keep it going. Now you have to figure what it will take to keep *you* going. It will be at least a year, if not more, before your business turns a profit. If you have quit a job to launch this enterprise, how much will you need to live on until you will be able to draw income from the business? Get your figures together and then go over them with your accountant, who will then prepare a balance sheet for fundraising presentation.

What Your Business Plan Must Include

1. *A description of the business and how it will make money*

Explain what you will sell and why you will sell a million of 'em. Describe the business, your product or service, and your business goals. Don't go wild; bankers and investors deal in reality. Explain who will buy your product and why, and how it is different and better than existing ones. It is especially impressive if you have a track record and can show that your product was tried and accepted; if you can get testimonials from satisfied users, that's even better. Outline your marketing strategy—how you expect to attract customers with advertising and sales promotion. Estimate the competition and explain how you expect to win a percentage of market share (a favorite buzzword that makes your business plan sound professional, especially when it's accompanied by a percentage figure; bankers love numbers). If there are technical aspects with which your lender or investor may not be familiar, outline them in detail. The more knowledgeable you are about your business, the more impressed they will be.

2. *Why you are qualified to launch and run this business*

If you plan to open an art gallery, the fact that you were an art major in college and have run art sales for your favorite charities would be important. Loan officers want to know that you have the knowledge, training, and experience to make a success of your business. When launching an enterprise, it is important to stress the skills you have and which ones you intend to buy by hiring consultants or employees. Management is a very important factor to loangivers; they need to have full confidence in your abilities and credentials.

3. *How much money you need and for what*

Outline exactly how the money will be used and why it is needed. This is the nitty-gritty stuff and is not something you can whip up yourself. Your accountant should prepare a chart of financial projections of expenses, sales, earnings, and cash flow on a monthly basis for the first two years, and on a quarterly basis for five years. It is an analysis that shows at what point money brought in by sales will break even with costs, and profits begin. No one expects a new business to make money for at least a year, if not two. The chart will show projected growth in sales and profits with an explanation of how this will come about.

Be sure you understand these projections. You have to be able to understand these numbers and discuss them with the bank when you talk to the loan officer. As one banker said: "It's important that people get professional help, but if a business person doesn't understand the dynamics of what she's doing, I get a little nervous."

4. *How much you are prepared to invest*

If you don't have enough faith in the project to put in your own money, why should they? Banks want to know that you are willing to put your money where your mouth is. If you believe so

strongly in the future success of this business, then you should
be expected to make some financial commitment. They usually
look for at least twenty-five percent, plus your signature to make
you personally liable for the loan. That means if the project does
not work out, for whatever reason, you will be held responsible
for repayment.

5. *How you want the loan structured*

What kind of loan are you looking for and how do you want it
set up? How many years do you want for repayment? You may
not get the arrangement you want, but this information demonstrates that you have thought out the financing process and are
knowledgeable about business finance.

How to Present Your Business Plan

Of course, there will be an interview because basically, it's you
they are buying. If you come to the interview equipped with a
full understanding of the industry you are planning to enter and
the business you wish to launch, if you demonstrate a good
grasp of the financial details, if you project belief in your enterprise and assurance that it will succeed, then they will be convinced.

When Dick and Maurice McDonald wanted to open a ham-
burger restaurant in San Bernadino, California, in 1937, they
needed $7,500 to get started. Every bank they approached asked
for collateral, which they didn't have. Finally, in desperation,
they decided to take a crack at a really big bank and went to the
Bank of America. Fully expecting to be turned away, they were
surprised to be granted an interview with the bank manager, who
listened carefully to their proposal and told them to return in a
week for the bank's answer. One week later, they nervously
came back. The manager told them that the finance committee
was not overly impressed with the idea but that he frequently
liked to play hunches, and he had a hunch that the McDonald

brothers would make it big. The bank could not extend a loan of $7,500, but would they find $5,000 acceptable? They did, and the rest is history.

The moral of the story is that banks and investors are just people, with varied opinions and feelings. They react to the same stimuli as you and I, and are as responsive to convincing arguments as everyone else. Remember, too, that they *want* to lend money because that's how they make money—by earning interest from loans.

The best way to bring someone over to your point of view is to first understand his point of view. Put yourself in *his* head to determine what kind of facts would impress him. If someone came to you for a loan, what would you want to know to assure you that you would get your money back with interest?

If you believe in your proposal, don't let a few turndowns turn you off. Go from bank to bank, and don't be afraid of the big ones; often they are the most sympathetic to new ideas. Keep at it, and you may find the one who has a hunch about you.

The SBA (Small Business Administration)

All this stuff you keep reading about how the government is positively dying to aid small business is very misleading. You get the picture of eager hands reaching out to help you start this wonderful enterprise that will make some small contribution to expanding the United States economy. So you figure that all you have to do is walk in to the Small Business Administration, plead your case, and walk out with a check—just like the episode of *Roseanne* when she wanted to open her own coffee shop.

Forget it. The SBA has no money. What they do is act as guarantors to the bank that lends you money, which is worked out between the bank and them. You furnish the bank with your business plan and adequate collateral, if the bank approves, they submit it to the SBA for processing. The SBA can guarantee ninety percent of a loan of up to $155,000 and eighty-five percent of a loan up to a maximum of $750,000.

They used to supply loans years ago, but budget cuts did away with their funds and today they've become more of an advisory than an active agency. The only direct loans they offer are to Vietnam veterans, the disabled low-income individuals, or businesses located in what the Department of Labor calls "labor surplus areas." In other words, if you wanted to open a business in a deprived area with a high unemployment rate where the government felt you could put some of the locals to work, and at least two banks turned you down, you would be considered for a direct loan.

However, they *can* help you with advice. When you plan to start a business, it's important to know all the rules and regulations of the field and the requirements of the town, county, state, and Federal governments. For instance, to have a landscaping business, you may need a county license of business operation as well as a pesticide license in order to purchase and dispense chemicals. Or if you plan to open a day-care center, there are stipulated legal and insurance requirements. Write to your nearest SBA branch, describe your business, and they will send you a kit that supplies you with information and guidance on that industry.

If you have little or no entrepreneurial experience, the SBA offers a service you might find extremely helpful. It's called SCORE, which stands for the Service Corps of Retired Executives. These are individuals who either ran their own businesses or worked at executive levels in big corporations and now freely offer the benefits of their expertise and experience to neophyte entrepreneurs. For more details on aid offered by the SBA, and other resources for free advice, call your local SBA and ask for the list of organizations in your area who offer help to launchers of small businesses—especially to women.

Women are "hot" these days, and not-for-profit groups to help women in business seem to be springing up daily. Beware.

Many of these seem to be not-for-anything except their own self-promotion. I called a few and got answers like "I'm busy now and there's nobody else here who can help you, so call back after 3 PM." When I finally reached someone who had finished giving herself a manicure, I was sent a package (incorrectly addressed to *Sandy* Smith) of brochures describing expensive seminars and conferences. These events typically offer morning coffee, luncheon, and cocktail reception, and feature keynote speakers (like Oprah Winfrey and Ivana Trump) who could probably offer great tips on dieting and cosmetic surgery but who seem somewhat unequipped to supply guidance on small business. Unfortunately, many women are finding this starting-a-business project to be a great fill-in fun activity to get them through those dull months between the tennis and ski seasons. If you want to regard it as a hobby, you can spend days and evenings socializing at meetings, seminars, and conferences.

If you are serious about starting your business, one good course or seminar, plus this book, should tell all you have to know. And there's no need to shell out big bucks for a seminar; watch the business pages of your local newspaper for listings of free presentations offered by banks, chambers of commerce, colleges, and small business organizations in your area. There are state, city, and often county Economic Development Agencies all over the country who are primed to help; check your local phone book. Your Chamber of Commerce may also offer assistance and guidance.

Your local utilities—the electric, gas, and telephone companies—are excellent sources for free guidance in starting a business. Before you get too impressed with their wonderful, altruistic community spirit, just think how helping establish new businesses that will need their services ultimately adds to their bottom line. Because they are private companies driven by the profit motive, they are usually better organized and more efficient than governmental or not-for-profit agencies, which means their help can be more effective.

7

The Launching:
Let's Get This Business
Off the Ground

What's in a Name?

You have probably been thinking of names for your business for
months. Everybody has suggestions for brilliant plays on words
that are sure to create instant admiration in the industry and in
your community.

Who needs admiration? What you want is sales.

Don't kill yourself with being clever. Those adorable names
so dear to novice businesspeople usually mean more to them
than to prospective customers. And chances are your clever
name has been thought of earlier by someone else, perhaps in a
related industry, and thus loses the edge you really need, which
is *distinction*.

For instance, have you ever noticed how many businesses in
the computer field have Micro or Compu in them? Or how
many plastics or glass businesses are called Kleer-Vu or Klear-
something? Or how many healthcare companies have Medic in
their names? How often have you seen words like Kwik and
Ezy in company or store names? Or cleaners called Kwik
Klean? My local phone book has fifty-nine beauty salons
named "Hair something": Hair Port, Hair Kraft, Hair We Are,
Hair Today, Hair 'N' Now....

You may come up with a name that you and your friends and family think is super-duper darling. It's descriptive, it's clever. But does it do its job?

The purpose of a name is to be *memorable*. When a prospective customer wants to phone you with an order, she should be able to remember your name easily, and not be confused by a million other soundalike names. What's wrong with your own name—either first or last, or both? Sara Lee did fine. Mary Kay, Johnson & Johnson, Procter & Gamble—the advantage of such names is they are unique and thus easier to remember.

Don't knock yourself out trying to find a name you think is suitable. It's far more attention-getting if it's unsuitable. Can you imagine the reaction of the staid, conservative computer industry when a brash young group of brilliant entrepreneurs came up with the unlikely name of Apple?

Don't make the mistake of including the specific business of the company in the name. This can be limiting to future growth. Many years ago when the Schapiras opened their now famous Schapira Coffee Company in Greenwich Village, they obviously never intended to sell teas as they do today. How many times have you seen a major corporation change its name because it is no longer apt to be called the so-and-so oil corporation when they have been expanding into other fields, especially if they acquire a food company. Wouldn't you find it a little off-putting to pick up a box of cereal and notice it is a product of the ABD Oil and Chemical Corporation?

Allow yourself room for future diversity by giving your company a name that can encompass many areas of growth. Avoid locking yourself into a specific service, product, or process. Kentucky Fried Chicken changed its name to KFC to avoid the stigma of "fried" foods in today's health-conscious market.

Create a Logo—Your Special Symbol

You have a distinctive-sounding name. Now you must make it distinctive-looking with your own logo.

A logo is a design that becomes visually associated with your company—the personal, unique symbol that distinguishes it. Sometimes it may be just the style of type your name will appear in always. Look at department store ads and note how store names always appear in a specified style; that is their logo. The company name may be enclosed in a shape such as an oval. Sometimes a logo is a symbol, like the peacock on NBC or the lion in MGM films, and is always displayed next to, above, or below the company name.

The logo appears on your stationery, ads, delivery vehicles, and signs. In a store, it appears on your windows, bags, boxes, and sales slips. If you're opening a restaurant, it appears on your menus.

Since this emblem will be displayed everywhere, it is important that it be as effective as possible. Needless to say, this is not a do-it-yourself project, nor some little job you turn over to your artistic friend who made some great signs for last year's rummage sale. This requires a professional graphic designer, who will create a look that is representative of your company and conveys an impression of the kind of business you are. If you intend to carry upscale merchandise, you want your logo to give a sense of elegance. If you are offering a business-to-business service, you want the feeling of no-nonsense efficiency. All of this can be created with a logo executed by a professional graphic designer. Be sure you tell the artist the feeling you wish to convey about the character of your company. Prudential's Rock of Gibraltar is good for the strength and dependability of an insurance company, but may not sit well with potential customers of, say, a lingerie shop.

Ask the artist to submit a few sketches of possible designs. Choose the one that pleases you, *then tell the artist to show you how the logo looks in different sizes.* She can reduce it and blow it up so that you can see how it looks in the many sizes in which it will appear, from small on envelopes and invoices, to large on packages and signs. You should expect to pay one thousand dollars, or more, for the services of a professional designer.

The Grand Opening (Let 'Em Know You're Here)

This is no time for being laid back. It's time to make noise, attract attention, and let the world of prospective customers know that you have arrived to offer them wondrous products and services they need and want.

The Kick Off Mailing

You must create a printed piece that describes your business and introduces you to your buying public. (Instructions on how to write and prepare direct mail appear in the following chapter.) Mail this piece or distribute it in other ways to all prospective customers and clients. How do you find them? That's easy. Look in your regional Yellow Pages under the heading "Mailing Lists," where you will find companies that offer lists of home-owners and businesses broken down into geographic and demographic categories.

If you are opening a retail store, decide upon the areas from which you can reasonably expect to derive trade and mail your literature to every resident of those communities.

If you are starting a business service and wish to reach all small businesses in your area, the local Chamber of Commerce may have available lists. However, chances are their list is of member companies only and is not broken down into categories that would be effective for you. For instance, if you are offering a service aimed at small businesses, there would be no purpose in having your mailing going to IBM-and General Motors-size companies. To get selective lists, you are probably best off with the list companies shown in the Yellow Pages.

Grand Opening Party

Call it an "Open House." Call it a "Grand Opening Gala." Call it whatever you want. But blast off with a big celebration to call attention to your arrival on the commercial scene.

Retailing

Run ads in the local papers inviting everyone to your opening party. Print fliers and post them in supermarkets or slip them under windshield wipers. Entice the buying public with offers of lovely freebies—cookies, candy, gifts, prizes, coffee, and cake. There are people who will come just because they're curious; others have to be lured by the appeal of free goodies.

Invite the Press: Talk to the advertising representative who sold you space in the local paper. Invite her, and tell her you'd like to also invite the editor to the festivities, along with a photographer. The reason I suggest you speak to the ad department before editorial is that, in small city newspapers, advertising has big clout and the fact that you are a paying advertiser assures editorial attention. This is not necessarily so in large cities where the two departments keep assiduously apart, and a call to the editor demanding he cover your news story because you advertise in the paper will insure a very cold shoulder indeed.

Invite Local Politicos: Politicians—the mayor, city council members and others—thrive on high visibility among the "people." If they think there will be a showing of their constituents, especially in an election year, they'll come. And if you tell them the press will be present, they'll be there for sure, especially if a photographer is on hand. Actually, it works two ways: the press is attracted to politicians, and politicians are drawn to the press. This symbiosis works for you because their attendance lends importance to the event.

First impressions are important, and this is your chance to put on the face you want customers to remember. Music is a nice touch. Show your support for the community by having musicians from the high school orchestra sitting in a corner playing classical music. A string quartet creates a lovely ambiance and adds elegance to the party. Be sure, of course, that the place looks spiffy and especially that you have a well-dressed window, which may call for professional window-dressing help (at least until you learn the technique).

If you are a food establishment, either a take-home or restaurant facility, this is the time to serve with what my mother used to call an "open hand." Portions should be generous. There is nothing that satisfies people more than feeling they are getting full value for their dollars. If in time you find that your profit margin is too slim, you can start to slowly—very slowly—cut back on serving sizes.

The "Grand Opening" party may be one day only, but the benefits of the occasion can be prolonged for promotional purposes by having "Grand Opening Month Specials" for the entire month.

Service or Manufacturing: If you have a well-furnished facility, lovely offices, and a well-equipped production plant, a "Grand Opening Party" can be an impressive event.

However, unlike a retail store where it's come-one-come-all and the aim is to pack the place with the general populace, here you should be selective. You must send out invitations to all potential customers and clients whom you wish to impress and convince them to deal with you. Offer an incentive for them to come, like a champagne reception (with tasty Cordeniu Spanish Champagne available at seven bucks a bottle or Andre at under four dollars, you can afford to put on the dog). I like to make it a breakfast, at which we make Mimosas (champagne and orange juice), thus cutting down on the champagne nicely. I also serve bagels and cheese, coffee and danish. Not only is the food service more economical, but I find you get a better turnout mornings because people come in before going to their offices and getting embroiled in the day's demands.

Otherwise, follow the same procedures as for a retail store. Invite the press, but you may have to phone the city desk editor directly since you may not be planning to do advertising. Invite the local politicians who will feel they must support new business by putting in an appearance. And have the string quartet. If the high school does not have musicians, try local colleges and music schools.

Include an RSVP card in your invitation so that you know in

advance how many people to expect, which is important when food service is involved.

The purpose of this "Grand Opening" is to introduce your business to the industry. If you are a manufacturer, then by all means invite representatives of the trade magazines of your industry. It is important to send everyone home with a reminder of the occasion. Prepare a press release that tells all about you and your company so that your guests not only have a ready-for-print article about the event but also your name, address, and phone number on hand for future contact. (For guidance on how to write and produce a Public Relations News Release, see the following chapter.)

8

Advertising and Public Relations: How to Get BIG Results From a SMALL Budget

From the moment you open your doors, salespeople from publications you never heard of will be calling you insistently to convince you of the vital importance of advertising in their newspapers and magazines.

If you have a retail store or a local service business, the area newspapers will give you dire predictions of the certain demise of your business if you do not let the community know of your existence by running big ads in their publications. If you have a manufacturing business, all the trade media advertising salespeople will assault you with charts and surveys to prove that theirs is the best in the field.

Hold off making any commitments until you know where, what, and when to advertise. Do not put one cent into advertising until you have taken the time to ascertain where to put your dollars in order to get the best possible value and results.

Advertising is invaluable when building a business, but unfortunately, it's the area that is most neglected by new entrepreneurs. This is understandable because you spend your days dealing with the myriad of details involved in running a business, and advertising is the intangible that can be most easily put off. As a result, like most small businesspeople, you can waste thousands of dollars by responding to high-pressure calls from ad salespeople who may sincerely believe in their publication, but who do not really understand if advertising in it will prove of value to you. It may sound like a great deal when you're told that your ad in a newspaper will be seen by hundreds of thousands. But what's the point of reaching thousands of readers of whom only ten percent are your potential customers? You will be paying for what is known as "waste circulation."

You wouldn't buy a car or a house without checking out the market to be sure you get the best product for the best price. Don't you think your advertising purchases should get at least the same level of research?

Rules for Getting the Biggest Bang for Your Advertising Buck

RULE 1. Target Your Market: How to find and reach your specific customers

The greatest, cleverest ad in the world wouldn't create a single sale unless it was read by people who need your product or service. Therefore, it is absolutely imperative that before you advertise you know exactly who is your potential customer so that you can then find the sort of publication she reads. In other words, you must make a *demographic profile* of the person to whom you expect to sell your product or services.

A *demographic profile*, as used in the advertising world, defines an individual by income, age, and education. For example, let's say you plan to open a store featuring expensive foods like caviar, truffles, and other luxury goodies. These are the demographics that would describe your probable customer:

> HOUSEHOLD INCOME—$60,000 a year and over
> AGE—35 and over
> EDUCATION—college and over

OK, now what do you do with this information? You look for a publication in your area that caters to this buyer. Advertising rates are based on readership. If you place ads in your local newspaper, you would probably reach some of these people but you would be paying for exposure to thousands of readers who would *never* enter your shop. You would get far more value for your dollar if you advertised in sophisticated magazines like *Time, Newsweek, Bon Appetit, House Beautiful,* and *Metropolitan Home.* I can just hear your gasps of disbelief as you wonder if I've gone off my rocker. How can I suggest to a new storeowner—who plans to live on pizza for a year in order to cover the rent—that she run an ad in *Time* where a four-color, full-page ad costs $120,000? It does sound off-the-wall, but I'm going to let you in on one of the best-kept secrets of the media-buying world: Magazine Networks Inc. (MNI) is an organization that sells space in regional editions of the top national publications. You can buy a full-page ad that will appear *only* in copies of *Time, Newsweek, Sports Illustrated, U.S. News and World Report, House Beautiful, Metropolitan Home,* and *Bon Appetit* that are mailed to subscribers in your area. One full page that appears in *all* five or six of these magazines can be bought for $3,500.

Think of the impressive effect. Every reader of these upscale magazines in your locality will see your ad right alongside ads for Jaguar, BMW, and AT&T. This subtly puts you in their class, which is the aim of all major media buyers who know the importance of having their advertising appear in the correct environment.

Think of how much more effective it is to be seen in this elite company than to have your shop featured in the local newspaper next to a garden center ad for a "Big Two-for-One Fertilizer Sellathon!" Just like people, businesses are known by the company they keep. Having your ad appear in a prestigious national magazine conveys an image of substance, solidity, and success that will bring in business.

As an additional bonus, you get the tremendous additional

value of merchandising aids supplied by MNI, such as reprints of your ads bearing the impressive line: "As Advertised in *Time*," *Newsweek*, etc. You can use these as direct mailers or as laminated counter cards mounted on an easel that you display in your window or on the counter.

I'll never forget the reactions MNI advertising created for the first client for whom we used it. It was a small but elegant menswear shop in Scarsdale that had been running ads in the local newspapers as well as the *New York Times* for years. As soon as our ads appeared in *Newsweek, Time, U.S. News & World Report*, and *Sports Illustrated*, new customers sought out the store, and old customers were awed. Where before they assumed the owner was just a small-town haberdasher, they now regarded him as a successful and sophisticated purveyor of men's clothing, and began to consult him respectfully for his opinion on style. People assume that if you can afford expensive advertising, you must be rich; and if you're rich, you must be successful; and if you're successful, you must be smart.

To get full details on MNI advertising, call or write for a media kit to:

Jack Mohan
MNI (Media Networks Inc.)
530 Fifth Avenue
New York, New York 10036
Phone: (212) 536–7845

There are thousands of publications in the U.S.: consumer magazines, trade magazines, and newspapers. To learn which ones are suitable for your business and how much they cost, go to your library reference room and ask for *Standard Rate & Data*, which comes in separate volumes for each of the categories mentioned as well as for radio/TV.

Don't overlook small local publications that may not be big enough to get a *Standard Rate & Data* listing, but may be ideal for you. For example, if you plan to start an employment service for law office temps, you would undoubtedly do well with ads in the local bar journal.

To get the fullest value out of your advertising investment, allocate a budget, analyze and select your publications carefully, and then map out an annual advertising schedule. Specify the exact dates of insertions for your high and low sales periods.

Do not allow yourself to be lured into what I called "gotta" advertising. That's when you succumb to frantic calls from ad space salespeople telling you about "special issues" covering your specific business that you just "gotta" be in because all your competitors will be present. Chances are they got them in by telling them that you'll be in. Let me give you a tip about "Special Issues": They are created by the publisher as a hook to bring in ad revenue and offer little benefit to advertisers.

RULE 2. Use Small Space Effectively: Frequency vs. Size

Since you are working with a small budget, you will have to make a choice between running a few big ads or a lot of small ones. It has proven far more effective to keep your name in front of the market as often as possible with smaller ads rather than hit them once in a while with big ones.

The reason is that you want to be there, in front of the buyer, at the "magic moment" when the prospect makes the decision to *buy*. Let's say you have a refrigerator that's on its last legs. You know it will need replacement soon, so you take casual note of ads for fridges. Then one night, the unit dies and it's panic time.

"What the devil was the name of that store that ran that big ad on appliances?" If their ad isn't there when you need it, you'll give your business to the store whose advertising you see at that moment. By keeping up a steady flow of ads, no matter what size, you are more likely to be visible at that magic moment when the customer is ready to buy.

RULE 3. Stick With One Publication Rather Than Scatter Your Ads

It's tempting to want to see your ads in many publications, but it's not good business when you're operating with a limited budget. *Repeating an ad in one magazine three times is far more productive than placing a single ad in each of three magazines.*

When you pick up a magazine in which you are an advertiser, you turn immediately to your ad. Naturally. It's yours so you read it carefully, and make the erroneous assumption that every reader has followed the same procedure. *Wrong.* Most people are flippers; they flip from page to page until they hit something that catches their immediate attention. It could be your ad, but chances are they pass it by with only subliminal note of its presence.

It will take at least three times before your ad impacts on their conscious awareness. Rather than spreading yourself thin with sporadic ads in different publications, select the one you feel will most effectively reach your constituency and hit away over and over so that they inevitably come to recognize your company name and product. Remember, if you want to fell a tree, you don't hit wildly at different spots; you keep swinging your axe in one place until the desired effect is achieved.

RULE 4. Repeat the Same Ad Over and Over

Take a tip from TV. How often do you see the same ad repeated over and over again, ad nauseam?

Don't be afraid to use the same ad for many weeks or months. It is not necessary to create a new ad for every insertion. Unfortunately, the advertiser usually has seen the art and copy so often during the creative process that by the time the ad appears, she's bored with it. There's a story about Henry Ford, who was presented with the printed final proof of a four-color ad to appear in the national magazines. He looked at it and then said to the advertising agency account executive, "I'm tired of this ad. Let's do a new one."

The account exec said, "But Mr. Ford, this ad hasn't run yet."

There's no need to incur the expense of creating and producing a new ad for each insertion. Keep repeating the same ad over and over again as long as it's effective and tells the story.

RULE 5. Take Advantage of Corporate Co-op Funds:
How to Get Someone Else to Pay for Your Advertising

It sounds like an entrepreneur's dream come true—someone else who is eager and willing to contribute toward your advertising expenditures.

It's real; it's available; it's there for the asking. Most manufacturers have a co-op advertising program that offers to pay in part for ads featuring their products. If you're a retailer, ask every one of the companies whose products you sell for co-op funding. If you're a manufacturer, or a service organization, ask every company whose products you use if they have co-op funding.

The usual procedure is that they will supply you with slicks, which are ready-to-print ads for their products with room at the bottom for your logo, name, and address. When the ad runs, you send them proof of insertion (tearsheet of the ad and copy of the publication's bill) and they will reimburse you for whatever portion they offer (usually fifty percent).

It's a wonderful deal. You have *no* production costs because they supply completed ready-for-camera material, and then they pay up to half of the space cost. It's a gift that enables you to get double the mileage from your advertising budget.

How to Write Ads That SELL

Have you ever admired an ad for its cleverness and stunning graphics but were not sure what product was being advertised? We of the small budget world cannot afford the luxury of running ads that evoke admiration but not sales. It is not hard to write copy that sells, nor does it take great genius. The important part of writing effective copy is evolving the right approach, the basic appeal that touches closest to the heart of the buyer. It is a distillation process, a careful analysis of the product or service you are selling and of the needs of the people who will be buying it.

Remember that you are not selling a product, you are selling a *benefit*. No one cares how gorgeous it looks, how carefully you made it, what a great bunch of people you are—they want to know "What benefit will I get from using this product? In what way will my life be made better if I buy it?"

> *STEP 1: Analyze your product or service.* Evaluate its features and list every conceivable service it performs for the user. For example, you have a laundry. You turn out finely finished work, you pick up and deliver, you replace missing buttons. You have a local gift shop. You carry a selective group of high quality items as well as an eclectic array of crafts.
>
> *STEP 2: Convert these assets into benefits.* The Laundry: You offer the benefits of convenience, more leisure time for the homemaker, a smoother home life. The Gift Shop: You offer the benefits of eliminating the wear and tear of going downtown to shop and the convenience of one-stop shopping for all your gifts.
>
> *STEP 3: Find the USP (Unique Selling Proposition).* Advertisers have learned that if you try to tell people everything about a product, they remember nothing. The only way to grab attention and be remembered is to feature *one* major benefit that the user will associate with your company. This is called the USP.
>
> The Laundry: "Let us *free* you for the better things in life." The Gift Shop: "The Right Gift, Right Here on Main Street."

These are just some suggestions to give you an idea of how to get your mind going. The purpose and power of a USP is that it enables the buyer to remember you by associating a single big benefit with your product. Just to give you an idea of the effectiveness of USPs, what do you think of when you hear Volvo? (Safety.) Rolex? (Impressively expensive.) Marlboro? (Macho.)

STEP 4. The hook to make them buy NOW. OK, you sold them. Now how do you make them get off the dime and call, or come in to the store? Reel 'em in with the hook that makes them feel they must respond immediately or lose a golden opportunity, like "Special 25 pecent discount for all orders received by October 30th" or "FREE GIFT when you bring in this ad."

Special Copywriting Tips

- **Don't Kill Yourself Being Clever:** Resist the urge to show off with witty play-on-words headlines. These may bring praise for your creativity, but will they bring sales? It's the promise of benefits that makes people buy.
- **Use Humor:** A light touch is lovely. It makes people smile, and that's always nice. Alka Seltzer has built a business on entertaining commercials.
- **Don't Use Corny, Cliche, Do-Nothing Words:** "Quality," "Dependability," "Economical," "Service": Since everybody, including your competitors, uses these same generalities, the words alone convey nothing distinctive about your product and are thus a waste of space. It is far more effective to specify a real-life benefit the buyer will derive from each of these features rather than just listing them. One of my students told us how her husband had gone to Sears intent on buying a $200 lawn mower and returned home with a fancy $700 machine.

"What ever made you spend so much?" she asked.

"This one had a tag on it that said 'Guaranteed to start with the first pull of the cord.'"

If the tag had borne the boring generality "Dependable," he would have passed it by. But the *specific* feature of dependability reminded him of the aggravation and strain of repeated yanks to get the old mower going, which hit a nerve and impelled him to go for the more expensive unit. Instead of "Economical," exactly how much will they save? As for the promise of "Service," exactly what do you do that's above and beyond what every other company offers? In what way will the high quality of *your* service benefit your customer?

- **Use Testimonials:** People are always impressed when they see that others have been pleased with your product or service.
- **Appeal to One or More of the Three Power-Pullers:** Play to the customer's Ego, Greed, and Self-Interest, and you can't lose.

Direct Mail—the "NOW" Medium

Any advertising pieces that are delivered by the post office—brochures, cards, catalogs—are called "Direct Mail". Unlike an ad which can pull responses for as long as the publication is current (a day, week, or month), direct mail must evoke immediate attention and results or it's dead. Rarely do people hold on to mailings; the usual procedure is to read it and respond at once, or to dump it. Unlike an ad which is surrounded by interesting news stories which keep the readers' eyes on the page, a direct-mail piece stands alone. Which means it had better be knock-'em-dead gorgeous to grab their attention and impel them to take the three vital steps:

1. Open it
2. Read it
3. Act

At first glance, your piece must look provocative enough to compel the recipient to open or unfold it; it must promise a benefit that no one can turn down; and it must make the offering so desirable and pressing that she will immediately return the order or response card, or call, or do whatever she is asked to do in order to take advantage of this great deal.

To produce such a mailing involves the cooperative creativity of copywriting and graphic design. You have just learned how to turn out strong, compelling copy. Now those words must be presented in an artistic framework.

Until a few years ago, you would have given the copy to a graphic designer who would make a layout, then produce camera-ready artwork by purchasing typography, pasting it in place on boards, then hand-drawing designs and art. Today, it's all done by computer at half the cost with software like Aldus Pagemaker. (For details on how to produce your direct mail with computer graphics, read the next chapter.)

To Whom Do You Mail: Using the Right Mailing List

You now know exactly who your customer is so it should be simple to reach her via mail. In time, you will develop your own list of customers and people who have responded to your ads. But at the outset of your business, you will have to buy a mailing list. Actually, you don't buy the list, you merely rent it for one-time use from any of the sources you have found in the Yellow Pages under "Mailing Lists" as described earlier. Outline your specific goals to the list company and they will advise you how to reach your mail marketing objectives.

A Newsletter—An Absolute MUST

A newsletter is not an option, it's a necessity. This is a pretty strong statement but I back it with years of experiencing the tremendous effectiveness of this very simple and inexpensive form of direct mail.

A newsletter is actually your own little newspaper. It should be filled with newsy, gossipy tidbits of interest to your customers and prospects and it should be sent with cyclical regularity (once a month or at least every forty-five days) to every name on your mailing list. For small companies, and especially retailers, it builds an intimacy with the reader that cannot be achieved with any other medium.

A newsletter allows you to speak of the unspeakable—pointing out, for instance, why buying from your sleazy cut-rate competitors is foolish and ultimately costly. You do this by telling about an actual customer who came to you after suffering the miseries of mishandling elsewhere, and how grateful she was for the wonderful way in which you corrected the errors and got them up and going. Fill the newsletter with case histories of people who have dealt with you and are ecstatically satisfied. People are basically nosy and they love to read about other people's experiences. Tell stories about unusual uses or situations involving your products or services. Give your readers tips on living, recipes for healthy dishes, even jokes.

The newsletter, in effect, is a mini-newspaper in which you are the sole advertiser. Its primary aim is to build readership by being entertaining and informative. Sprinkled casually throughout the pages can be your propaganda—little plugs for your products and services. Don't hit them over the head with these messages, though; weave them gently and subtly among the general material.

Produce the newsletter yourself with desktop graphics (see computer chapter), or have it done outside. It offers a great way to solicit business subtly. Your newsletter will keep your name before customers and prospects so that when that "magic moment" for buying comes, they will instantly think of you.

Public Relations: How to Get Your Name in the Papers FREE

Contrary to popular conception, journalists and editors are just folks. And being ordinary people, they are basically lazy and looking for the easy way to get their work done. They need information from you to fill their pages and they'd just as soon not work too hard to get it. Which is why you must send them well-written, professional looking PR news releases detailing newsworthy happenings in your company. If it is truly news (and not some flimsy trumped-up hype like the three-man company who kept exchanging executive titles so that they could send in news releases about a "new executive appointment" every month) and is written like one of their regular news stories which requires them to do a minimum of editing work, it will make it into print.

How to Prepare a PR News Release

Suppose a wicked king ordered you executed but permitted you a last-minute plea for your life, providing your presentation was interesting and entertaining. But as soon as you lost his attention, you lost your head.

You would pour out vital facts and your most convincing arguments fast, right? You wouldn't save any goodies for later, because there might not *be* a later.

That's just the way you must think when writing a news release. The editor had better know the major points of vour story immediately or you'll lose your audience; ramble, and she'll stop reading. A properly written PR release, just like a newspaper story, has all the salient points up front. Supporting facts and the descriptive detailing come later.

You are fighting a battle to capture and hold the editor's inter est. The moment you become vague and imprecise, the second you go into hyperbole and overstatement, you'll lose her.

Who, What, When, Where, Why: The prime rule in journalism is that the opening paragraph of a news article must contain the answers to these five questions: Who? What? When? Where? Why?

The assumption is that the reader may never get past the first paragraph and you want to be sure she gets all the facts before she takes off.

This is exactly how you must set up your news releases. Bear in mind that the editor will have to convert your release into a news article; consequently, the less rewrite work you give an editor by closely adhering to proper journalistic form, the greater the chance that your release will be used. Remember, too, that this is not an ad. You cannot put in adjectives about the beauties and wonders of your product which are merely expressions of your opinion; this is supposed to be news and we want "just the facts, ma'am." However, you can slip in a little hyperbole by attribution: Just say "According to Joan Jones, president of Creative Kitchens Inc., 'We offer the largest selection of fine all-natural foods in the county.'" In that way, the editor doesn't take responsibility for the veracity of the claim but is merely reporting that Joan Jones said it.

What Should be Publicized: What should be the subject of publicity releases?

- *A new product or service* - anything new you are doing or producing.

- *An unusual sale* - Yoko Ono walked into your sportswear shop and walked out with $5,000 worth of gear for her upcoming mountain-climbing trip in Nepal. You did a landscaping installation for the Sheik of Abu Dhabi's beach house in your area, including $50,000 worth of palm and date trees to replicate his native environment. Editors love these kinds of glamorous human-interest stories.

- *Grand opening* - Tell them about the party and invite the press, which will insure media coverage of the event.

How to Create News When Nothing is Happening: Make a prediction about the future of your industry. (By the year 2,000, according to the traffic in yours and other take-out food shops, you foresee that 85% of American families will be eating take-out food at least three times a week.) Do a survey. (According to a survey of store traffic, 93% of Americans are dining on ethnic foods they never ate in their childhoods.) Making a prediction is not an exact science, so don't be afraid; you're entitled to express your opinion.

How to Spread the Word Across the Nation: If your product or service will be sold in locations throughout the country, you should get hold of *Bacon's Publicity Checkers*; they're available in most library reference rooms. These handy volumes list every magazine and newspaper in the U.S. and Canada according to category, with addresses, phone numbers, names of editors, and profiles of the publications so that you know if they're suitable for you. If you want to do a mass mailing and don't have the time to handle the effort yourself, they will do it for you. If you plan to do a lot of PR, you might want to buy your own copies. For information, call Bacon's at 800–621–0561.

9

Computers: A Small Business's Best Friend

It's an age thing. If you're under forty-five, computers are probably a familiar part of your life. But if you are older—fifty, sixty, or more—and have not been part of the work force for years, chances are the very word "computer" makes your eyes glaze over and the thought of using one makes you run for the Dramamine.

"Everyone tells me computers are wonderful, but what do I need one for? A typewriter works fine."

Equating a computer with a typewriter is like comparing a Cuisinart with a knife; the knife cuts but needs you to do the work, the Cuisinart cuts and performs many other important chores all by the press of a button. When you are buying basic equipment for your business, there's no point in wasting money on a single-function machine like a typewriter when, for not much more, you can buy a computer that not only types but also fulfills dozens of other important business needs, and will ultimately *save* you a great deal of money.

According to Ginny Pannier, a computer consultant in New York City who handles many small businesses and start-up situations: "Using a typewriter is painful always, but a computer is just painful at first and then the pain goes away."

She points out the difficulty of editing copy on a typewriter; misspellings are a nuisance to fix, and revisions require a total redo. Whereas typewriters correct only the errors you spot, the computer not only does that at the touch of a button, but also corrects errors and typos you weren't aware of with built-in spell-checkers and grammar-checkers to insure that your finished document is accurate in every way.

The choice is simple: If you are starting a business, you should start out with a computer.

I can just hear your groans: "But it seems so complicated. I read the ads for computers that describe all the things computers do, and it's like they're speaking another language."

They are, but don't let it throw you. First, you'll pick up the lingo soon enough. Second, you don't have to be concerned about and confused by *everything* the system does because you'll probably never use many of the functions. I have a food processor that included two attachments I have never even taken out of the box. My car offers a cruise-control feature that I will never use. The fact is, most equipment comes with one prime function for which we have bought it, and offers a slew of secondary functions which we will probably never use. That is how you should view your computer.

You will find that you'll use your computer constantly as a typewriter, checkbook manager, and bookkeeping ledger. Once you have gotten familiar with it, you may choose to expand its use. By then not only will you find it easy to move on to other functions, but I guarantee that you will have become so fascinated with your computer's capability to do things that save you time and aggravation that you will become hooked. That's what happened to me. Once I began to look upon my computer as a simple helper rather than a complicated machine, and started to use it for things other than word processing, I became an enthusiast. When I saw it reconcile my checkbook automatically with each entry, eliminating my monthly struggle to balance the numbers, I felt like an idiot for not having taken advantage of its features before.

To put you on the road to computer literacy, let me try to demystify all the gobbledygook terminology. The computer itself is called the "hardware." A complete computer system consists of four pieces: the screen (called the "monitor"); the keyboard, which is set up like a typewriter; the CPU (Central Processing Unit), which is the mechanism that runs the whole shebang; and the printer, which automatically types on paper whatever you have written on the computer. What makes the computer do things is the "software," which are discs that instruct the hardware. The hardware is the big one-time purchase. After that, when you want your computer do more, you'll buy different software packages that run from twenty-five dollars to a few hundred dollars. At the outset, all you need is basic software that will tell the computer to be used as a typewriter (now called a "word processor"). This same software will also contain the ability to instruct the computer to perform other functions, but you can get into that later on when you have become familiar with the system.

When you are starting a business, your major concerns are sales and expenses. Ms. Pannier advises her clients to hold off getting into more elaborate and costly software until they know exactly what jobs they need the computer to perform, and they can afford to devote the time to learning how to use it.

"At the beginning, you're better off using your energy on the skills and talents that brought you into the business, and putting all your efforts into building sales."

Ms. Pannier pointed out the case of a client who started out with a computer for word processing use only.

"Until we knew what computer help the business needed, and the principals had established the business to the point where they could take time to learn how to use the system, I felt it was foolish and wasteful to invest in software. Until that time, I provided computerized services like invoicing and payroll on my computer. As they became more established, I gradually moved specific tasks into their offices."

When you are embarking upon an enterprise, it's prudent to spend your money on basic expenditures only until you know the business will make it. I have seen people set up new businesses as though they're planning to become General Motors within a month. The elaborately decorated offices furnished with a fortune in the latest equipment are explained with the faulty rationale: "It's important that we start out right and ready to handle growth."

The trouble with that reasoning is (1) you've deprived the business of valuable capital that might be needed to keep it afloat during the slow start-up period, and (2) you're spending money to prepare for growth that may never come and elaborately equipping a business that may not last.

If there were an accurate crystal ball for business there would be no bankruptcy laws. No one can predict the success or failure of any enterprise; it takes at least six months to get a sense of whether or not the project has a future, and at least one to five years to see if the rosy future has panned out. Give yourself and the business between three and six months before you start adding to your computer system.

How to Computerize Your Business: Step by Step

The best procedure is to start with basic equipment and then move up as you grow. Here's a recommended purchasing pace to follow so that you will gradually become an efficiently computerized business.

STEP 1. Shop for a Computer

Like cars, there are new models every year and you can save a bundle by buying last year's model off the floor at the end of the year. Don't go for the most up-to-the-minute system that the salesman pushes because it has all the latest bells and whistles, most of which are too sophisticated for you to use. You should be able to get a complete computer system including the printer for between $1,500 and $2,000, depending on the number of competitive stores that exist in your area. If your area doesn't have many computer vendors, you can call some of the computer companies who will discuss your needs and sell and ship directly to you.

STEP 2. *Software for Word Processing/Typing*

There are many brands of software to do typing and basic office work. I prefer PFS: First Choice® by Spinnaker, which costs about $45. It's very easy to use for word processing and it does everything I need to produce letters, reports, copy, and all the usual typewriter functions. It costs a lot less than some of the others, like WordPerfect® and is far less complicated and simpler to learn. I'm one of those unmechanical types who freezes at using any tool more complex than a screwdriver, and it took me about two hours with the User's Guide that comes with the package to learn how to use it.

First Choice® also gives you other functions such as a database, which is computerese for record card listings. It enables you to keep a handy up-to-date file of your customers, complete with their latest activities and purchases. You merely type in a "file card" on which you fill in each customer's name, address, when you saw her last, what she bought, and whatever details are important for you to track. You type in updated activities as they occur. Instead of keeping an index file in a box, the "cards" sit conveniently in your computer. This database feature makes it easy for you to compose letters to these customers with merely a press of a button.

STEP 3. *Software for Checkbook and Financial Management*

Like every businesswoman, I had a bookkeeper. I paid her a pretty steep hourly rate to handle and track our accounts payable and accounts receivable. She wrote checks and entered each expense under the proper debit heading; she recorded payments from clients and then calculated the balance so that I knew how much money we had in the bank at all times. She sent ledger sheets to our accountant, who prepared the necessary quarterly reports. I *had* a bookkeeper. Now I have Quicken® by Intuit.

These days, anyone who has a half-hour free (including unmathematical types like me) can sit down once a week at the computer and do the bookkeeping; you just type in the name of the payer or payee and the amount, and Quicken® types the checks, does the arithmetic and accounting. Every three months, Quicken® prints up a quarterly statement that goes to our accountant. Later on, you may want to go into the more advanced Quickbooks®, which does invoices, payroll, and many other accounting functions.

STEP 4. *Software to Help You Sell*

You made a sales call on a prospect some time last month. Is it time to contact her again, and what was the item she showed special interest in? Your life is a constant whirl of sales calls and it's impossible to remember who you saw when and to recall what transpired during each visit. But in order to build a business, you not only must keep track of all sales leads and sales calls, but keep in constant contact with prospects in order to develop them into customers, and with customers to keep them buying. You need what is called a "contact management" aid.

You could keep a handwritten notebook or Rolodex record, but they will become dog-eared and illegible. You could also make your breakfast toast in the broiler and watch it to prevent burning, or use an automatic pop-up toaster. When a product has been designed to do a specific job faster, better, and more effectively, isn't it foolish not to take advantage of its existence? What you should get is a contact management software package, like ACT!® by Contact Software International.

This kind of system—and there are a number of them at various prices dependent upon their capabilities and sophistication—enables you to keep up with, and on top of, leads and customers quickly and efficiently. ACT!®, and similar packages, will summon up a complete history of every client, customer, and prospect in seconds. It will help you to maintain a schedule of callbacks so that you don't have to try to remember when to remind each prospect about your product or service, and remind you to advise customers when it's time to reorder. It even provides a selection of stock form letters for all situations that you can turn out quickly and easily to keep in touch with customers and prospects.

STEP 5. *Software for Desktop Publishing*

The more often prospects and customers hear from you, the more often you will get business from them. When I was the advertising director of a company, I noticed that every mailing created a perceptible increase in incoming orders. But in those days, mailings required artists, typographers, and printers, and were too expensive to send out frequently. These days, you have software that enables you to turn out attractive direct mail and great-looking newsletters all by yourself.

Publish It!™ by Timeworks is a fairly simple package that gives you everything you need to produce professional-looking pieces right at your own desk on your computer. It contains complete, finished, ready-to-use cartoons and illustrations to put in wherever you want; you can create boxes, circles, all sorts of shapes to make the pages look attractive. Later on, when your business has grown and you want to have more elaborate and frequent mailings, it may pay to hire a person to produce them with software called Aldus Pagemaker®, which enables anyone to turn out stunning and distinctive brochures and catalogs.

STEP 6. *Software Specific to Your Industry*

There is software available that has been tailored to the needs of almost every business. The package for dentists will list all possible dental treatments, handle billing, and keep patient histories. Software for electrical wholesalers provides for inventory maintenance of specific electrical products. After you have your basic typing and financial management under computer control, it's time to check out the various software available specifically for your industry. There's no need to reinvent the wheel and knock yourself out creating a system for your business when it alrea exists. Here are some specific examples:

Software for Estimating: If your business requires constantly making estimates of jobs, and supplying quotes and bids, Estimator Plus® by ComputerEasy is a good addition to your software collection.

If you are a caterer, landscaper, estate appraiser, or in any business where you must consider a great number of elements and factors in costing out a job, preparation of an estimate takes a tremendous amount of time and painstaking effort. You can cut that time down to almost half by using a computer software system package like Estimator Plus®.

Software for Creating Layout Plans and Floorplans: If you do catering, landscaping, or interior design, Floorplan® by ComputerEasy enables you to lay out your design and prepare easy-to-read charts for prospects. Included are little drawings of trees, shrubs, doors, windows, and furniture that you can rearrange on your computer monitor in seconds.

There are software packages for your business that can make your life easier. Everyone who owns a business thinks her problems are unique and that no one else *really* understands how things must be done. Not so. Software has been created by individuals who made studies of your exact procedures and figured out how they can be done automatically instead of manually. To find out what software exists for your particular industry, your best sources are your trade publications and trade association.

SPECIAL NOTE: "WINDOWS"
When buying software, be sure to ask for the "Windows" version. This feature makes your computer easier and actually even fun to use.

10

To Grow or Not to Grow, That Is the Question

It's so nice to work at home. No commuting. Snacks and lunch are immediately accessible. You're there when the kids come home, and the tax deductions are a joy. You really don't want to move.

Then don't. One of the glories of the Computer Age is that it permits a small central office to operate efficiently with a large nonresident staff who work in their own homes on their own computers, communicating with (or in computerese, "interfacing with") the main office computer. This may sound complex and costly, but it isn't: all it requires is an inexpensive attachment called a modem. I once had a talented copywriter who wrote on her home computer and then sent the material through to my office computer. She had family demands at home that ordinarily would not have permitted her to take a job, but this method enabled her to work for me.

This practice has become so popular today that it has a name; it's called telecommuting. It's even used by Fortune 500 companies, who find they can cut down on costly office space by having employees work at home, and it also enables the companies to draw upon a large skilled workforce of part-timers who want or need to work at home.

If your business has grown to the point where your quarters seem cramped, don't jump to the conclusion that you must move into a larger space. First ask yourself: How much more business will we have to do just to cover the added overhead, and will it be worth the move? Are we getting the best value out of our current space or can we rearrange our floor plan in order to give us more efficient working conditions? And now the real moment-of-truth question: Am I moving to improve our facilities or to enhance my ego by having a glitzy office?

Should you expand or should you not? It all depends on your goals and your type of business.

Retailing

On Saturdays, and many evenings, your shop is standing-room-only. You look at the crush of customers happily and then worry that you may be losing business because of the crowded conditions. Should you move to a vacant, larger store around the corner? Should you wait until the little store next door is available so that you can expand? Should you open a second store?

First, you had better decide whether more space is what your kind of customer wants. A crowded store pulls in people because they assume you must be offering tremendous values if you can attract such a mob. Wide open spaces and big aisles are fine if you're selling $1,500 leather belts and $700 shirts and the customers demand a certain level of luxurious ambiance, but it's often a deterrent to budget-conscious shoppers. People love to feel they are buying bargains; many stores have built their success on crowded racks and counters, giving shoppers the exhilarating challenge of locating a real "find" amidst the junk, or often just creating the illusion of such a possibility. Look at all those exclusive antique shops that are so jammed you don't dare carry a shoulder bag for fear it will nudge a thousand-dollar vase off its pedestal. Before you spread out, you had better evaluate and analyze your customer base to see if more comfortable shopping conditions will work as a turn-off or a turn-on.

Perhaps you want more space to introduce a new level of merchandise in your store; maybe you want to bring in higher-priced lines. You've noticed well-dressed customers coming in to buy your featured stock of jeans, T-shirts, and other casual-wear items, and you've wondered if you couldn't derive more sales from the same traffic by offering them the expensive sports clothes they're now buying elsewhere. This is when it's a good idea to wait until the little store next door becomes available where you can create a luxury boutique annex that is convenient for customers to sashay into after buying jeans, and is easy for you to supervise. This is a good way to expand into a new market by dipping your toe in the water before making the big plunge.

A shrewd storekeeper in my area did just that and found he was getting almost double the amount of business from the same traffic he had before. Then he began to realize he was making more money far more easily on sales of expensive designer clothing. He also learned of the imminent arrival nearby of the Gap and other jeans-and-T-shirt stores. So he phased out his low-priced sportswear and, with minimum inconvenience to the large following he had developed, moved three doors down to open a posh, superbly appointed shop that has become one of the most highly successful high fashion stores in the area.

It's a good idea to get more out of your existing store traffi by expanding your lines horizontally, incorporating other cate gories of goods that appeal to your customers and are consonan with your image. But don't try to expand your merchandise vertically. In other words, just because you sell shoes it doesn't mean you can sell *all* kinds of shoes. When it comes to clothes, the elegance level is all important and changing it suddenly can be disastrous.

Some years ago, the head of a successful chain of low-priced shoe stores in Milwaukee thought he could increase business without increasing overhead by setting up a high-priced department in each shop. He figured he could reach a whole new market of buyers with a minimum of risk investment. Of course, it was a total fiasco because he never thought to analyze the buying psyche of upscale customers who could never be induced to spend $250 for a pair of designer leather shoes that shared shelf space with $30 manmade clunkers, nor consider being seen carrying packages bearing a store name that was renowned as "el cheapo." If it were just a matter of selling different kinds of shoes to his regular customers, it might have worked. But he tried to sell different kinds of shoes to totally different customers.

Now we come to the moment when you sit down quietly and introspectively determine your goals. Do you love your life as it is or do you want to build an empire? Growth inevitably means increased responsibility, greater challenges, and a major role change. It involves the added burden of more employees, higher rent, larger inventory, and the exciting but nerve-wracking decision to buy thousands of more dollars worth of goods that will require stepped-up sales promotion and advertising. It also means a change in your daily role, from a pleasant, sociable out-front proprietor to a beleaguered behind-the-scenes administrative executive. These are the personal decisions you must make before expansion.

The business decisions require different analyses and criteria. If you move around the corner, is it as good a location as you have now or is it off the main drag with poor visibility and parking accessibility? As for opening a second store, that's a whole new ballgame. A branch store means you will have to be in two places because absentee management doesn't work at the beginning. A bigger store will probably require a small bank loan, which should be fairly easy to get since you have a successful establishment. A second store would impose more serious financial demands: however, if you are ambitious and want to build an empire, it could be the beginning of a chain. As long as you understand the ramifications of expansion, the decision is up to you.

Manufacturing and Distributing

In this kind of business, you may not be able to choose whether or not to expand; prevailing conditions might force the decision. When you have a sales force, distributors, and manufacturers reps, their goal is to increase sales in order to increase their incomes. The toughest part of their jobs is introducing a new product or line; they are willing to invest the time and effort because they anticipate a future payoff in big volume sales once the product has been accepted. You cannot expect them to put in all that initial effort and then pull the rug out from under them with the sudden announcement, "Sorry fellas, we can't handle any more orders." If you put a limit on your output, thus limiting their sales, they'll be gone in a shot.

However, if you want to keep down the size of your company for whatever reason—maybe because of prevailing family responsibilities, or because you enjoy a business style that gives you the ability to maintain close personal supervision—you can control growth by selling your product regionally rather than nationally. Take on only East Coast or Midwest or Southwest or West Coast distributors and reps, thus putting limits on your output without putting limits on your sales people. When your personal situation and attitude change, you can then move into the other markets on a sort of grow-as-you-go plan.

Service Business

This kind of business gives you the greatest number of growth options. These days, you can run a business from home and expand easily and economically with the use of freelance help. Also, you can feel perfectly comfortable going after and getting big clients without feeling handicapped by your lack of fancy offices. Two factors have changed big company perceptions of home businesses—the recession and telecommuting. The recession forced many out-of-work top flight executives and creative people to start their own businesses at home, and the prevalence of telecommuting made dealing with home-working personnel an everyday affair. Home businesses are no longer looked down upon as small time mom-and-pop operations but are merely regarded as efficient, and you are judged today by what you do, not where you do it.

Many years ago, when my husband and I started an advertising agency in the playroom of our Scarsdale split-level, we were considered an oddity and were regarded with skepticism and shock by colleagues and friends. We did it because first, I am a risk-taker and second, we had clients before we even opened our doors. Of course, we were not neophytes; he had sold out his interest in the advertising agency he had started, but had grown to hate as it grew in size, and I was the former advertising manager of a company which would be one of our first clients. We felt we did not have to impress our clients since they knew us and were buying our proven talents, and we certainly didn't have to impress vendors. However, we did not want to look like we were living behind the store, so we moved to an all-glass house in the middle of two acres in Rye, a suburb easily accessible to New York City, the heart of the advertising world.

After our first month of operation, my husband was delighted to realize that he had earned more income from our little two-person firm than he had for a similar period from his thirty-five-employee New York City agency. The difference was, of course: *no overhead*. I'll never forget the stunned look on the face of the vice president of a major New York ad agency when he visited us for the first time. We had become acquainted with him and his wife on a Caribbean vacation. Over postprandial piña coladas, we discovered we were all in the advertising business and he asked the name and location of our agency. When we told him we worked out of our home, his expression of condescension (with a soupçon of pity) indicated he figured we had busted open our piggy bank to pay for the trip. Upon our return, we invited this couple over for dinner. As he walked into our house, his mouth fell open.

"You can live like this from your small agency? Hell, I probably bill out more in a day than you bill in a month!" I smiled at him sweetly. "Yes, but we keep it all."

With a service business, you can stay cozily at home and grow bigger without adding overhead. You just make more profit and the beautiful part is you get to keep it all.

11

Choosing Your Business: What Do You Have to Sell?

Now that you know you want to go into business, and feel confident that you can run it successfully, it's time to decide what kind of business you should start.

You may already have something in mind, a project that involves marketing a personal skill or interest. If you don't have a clue about where or what to start, don't make the mistake of plunging into just anything. The Skills-You-Can-Sell Conversion Chart should help you find a business for which you are eminently qualified and will enjoy.

"I'd love to start my own business, but what can I do? Maybe I'll open a shop. You don't need any sort of talent for that."

How many little boutiques have you seen come and go in your area started by misguided women who felt this way? They made the mistakes of miscalculating the demands of retailing, and underestimating their own ability to create businesses for which they are well-prepared.

Remember what I said earlier about your amassed expertise as the Chief Executive Officer of that hectic enterprise called

"The Home?" Well, now it's time to show you how those varied home-based activities have equipped you with salable qualifications that have great value in the commercial world. The Skills-You-Can-Sell Conversion Chart will give you ideas on how to use these specific talents to start your own business. To prove that it can be done, read the following success stories of eleven women who used their various areas of expertise to build flourishing enterprises. You may identify closely with some of their activities, or have other talents that you can convert into successful businesses just as they did.

It's important to choose a business that you will love and enjoy. If you don't really care about the product or service you are selling, your business will fail because you will never be able to convince customers to buy. An unenthusiastic salesperson is an inept one; and it's not just sales that will suffer. If you do not have a deep belief in your business, you will not be able to convey the confidence needed to deal effectively with banks, landlords, suppliers, and vendors. So choose a business you will truly enjoy. If you don't look forward to going to work every day, what's the point of it all? Remember how much of your life will be spent in this business of yours . . . how many hours of the day you will be there. On the scale of life priorities, your business should come right after your family in importance.

Special Events Marketing: Ann Tucker

Everyone congratulated you last year on the great job you did handling the big Spring Fair fund drive to buy the local hospital an MRI for its Radiology Department. It was even better than the tremendously successful PTA flea market you organized to buy new equipment for the school computer lab. You deserve all the accolades because bringing off a special event takes prodigious effort and coordination. Now wouldn't it be great to get cash as well as commendation for all your work?

The experience and abillty that made these events major suc-

THE SKILLS-YOU-CAN-SELL

Thirty skills that can be converte

Your Skills and Experience *(Activities you have been involved in for years)*	Your Commercial Potential *(Businesses you can build with these skills)*
1. Running charitable events	Special events marketing
2. Interested in antiques	Antiques show management
3. Serious collecting of a specific antique category	Exhibitor at antiques shows
4. Creating unique recipes	Food product manufacturer
5. Gourmet cooking	Gourmet foods sales to stores and restaurants Catering Opening a restaurant Opening an Inn
6. Running rummage sales, selling contents of family homes	Tag sale management
7. Gardening and landscaping homes and businesses	Landscaping service for
8. Writing	Publishing a newspaper
9. Doing publicity for local organizations	Public relations
10. Excellent design sense	Marketing home furnishings
11. Furnishing offices	Office design consultant for small businesses
12. An eye for decorative details	Gift shop Lampshade shop Bed-and-bath shop
13. Collecting period furniture	Used furniture & consignment shop

CONVERSION CHART

into forty-five viable businesses

14.	Collecting art	Art gallery
		Picture framing shop
15.	Refinishing furniture	Refinishing and restoration shop
16.	Style sense	Women's clothing store
		Accessories shop
		Lingerie shop
		Children's wear shop
		Costume jewelry shop
17.	Collecting antique clothes	Clothing consignment shop
18.	Sports enthusiast	Golf, tennis, and ski clothing shop
19.	Fitness enthusiast	Fitness & aerobics studio
20.	Fine baking	Bakery
21.	Fine cook	Take-out food shop
22.	Great partygiver	Party planner
		Party shop
		Wedding consultant
23.	Collecting old quilts	Quilt shop
24.	Skilled in needlepoint	Needlepoint shop
25.	Skilled in knitting	Knitting shop
26.	Skilled in sewing	Sewing shop
	Fabrics store	
27.	Making your own clothes	Couturier custom shop
28.	Animal lover	Pet shop
		Pet grooming
29.	Flower arranging	Florist shop
		Silk and dried floral arrangements shop
30.	Avid reader and booklover	Book shop

cesses can be the basis of a very lucrative and in-demand business, like the one started in 1983 by Ann Tucker.

"I parlayed a volunteer career into a business," she said as she sat in her home office with six women employees working away on phones, computers, and stuffing envelopes.

When Ann's volunteer job as executive director of child care at her church came to an end, she looked around for another avenue for her energy, experience, and well-honed organizational skills. A woman she knew had created a highly successful business, coordinating and managing events for the county. Ann called her for advice, and in effect asked, "Couldn't I do what you do?"

The friend was encouraging but unable to offer tangible help at the time. However, the query paid off months later when she phoned Ann to tell her of a real estate developer who needed someone to coordinate a special event promotion. Since private industry was not her bailiwick, she thought Ann might want to take it on. Armed with nothing more than confidence, Ann pitched for—and got—the assignment. This was the project that launched A.M. Tucker and Company.

"I worked forty-eight hours a day for three weeks," she told me with a smile.

Her efforts paid off. The event was a tremendous success, and Ann had a highly satisfied client who touted her talents to other businesses in the area. Recommendations brought more and more clients; Ann had found a niche that needed filling and soon A.M. Tucker and Company was firmly established in special events management, a fairly new field that has become so important today that New York University and other educational institutions offer courses and even certificates in it.

Ann had been working at home, but when the business grew to twelve employees, she felt it was time to move into offices nearby. Then, five years later, two critical occurrences took place that required a rearrangement of her life: her elderly father moved into her home and her teenaged son had a cancer operation that required a year of recuperation. Taking advantage of the unique flexibility offered by having your own business, Ann moved the company back into her home and pared her permanent personnel down to six; temps and subcontractors were hired when needed. Five years later, the company is one of the most highly-regarded events management organizations in the county.

To give you an example of what running an event management business entails, here's what happened when the National Council on Alcoholism and Other Addictions asked A.M. Tucker and Company to run a "Home Showcase" fund-raiser. This sort of project involves finding an empty mansion and getting local architects, interior designers, and landscapers to showcase their talents by decorating assigned rooms and areas. Thereby the mansion becomes a spectacular display of artistic creativity, drawing viewers—who pay hefty admission fees—by the busload.

"We worked for a full year on planning and preparation to get the project up and running," said Ann. "We tell clients all the strain and pain will be in our office, not theirs. We take care of everything down to the last minute detail."

Think of all the people and elements to be coordinated! You need to get permits from local authorities and neighbors; locate and sign up participating designers; arrange for shipping their furniture, paints, tools, wallpapers, shrubs, and plants to and from the Showcase House; set up transportation and parking facilities; and find and train volunteer guides to show visitors around. And, most important, you have to get the news out to the paying public to insure heavy traffic for the event, which means extensive mailings to prospective attendees as well as ads and publicity in local newspapers.

This hugely complex event went off with the seemingly effortless smoothness that is the mark of excellent management. The result: 11,000 people attended and the charity made a net profit of $100,000.

Developing a special events management business requires building a client base. As your reputation grows, they will come to you, but in the meantime you can't just sit around on your duff waiting for the phone to ring. You have to get out there and hustle for business by thinking up ideas for events for which you find suitable sponsors. For example, one of Ann Tucker's employees told her about the Pre-Christmas Festival of Trees sale that's a big annual event back in her hometown in Ohio. The trick in this business is to match the concept to the client; Ann brought the idea to the Red Cross and they said "Great." That was Step One. Then came the search for corporate sponsors. Having developed the sophisticated fund-raising strategy needed to attract corporate funding, Ann convinced Texaco to bankroll the event and persuaded a manufacturer of artificial flowers to donate wreaths and trees. The first Festival of Trees sale, with proceeds going to the Red Cross, was held in a local hotel and was such a hit that it has become an annual event with attendance building yearly.

Today, Ann Tucker lives and works in a lovely house in an estate area, complete with swimming pool and acreage. Her reputation brings in the steady flow of business that is the hallmark of a substantial, well-established company, but her success did not happen overnight. There are those who would say that Ann was lucky to be in the right place at the right time, but I say luck is only in the eye of the beholder. I believe in the "conveyor belt theory of life," which states that during the course of every person's lifetime, a steady stream of opportunities present themselves. The individual who has the perception to recognize the big chance, the sense to reach out and grab it, and the guts to take the risk of acting upon it, will be successful. Those who pass up the opportunities that continue to pass them by will always enviously attribute other's success to luck. Like every successful entrepreneur, Ann Tucker made her own luck.

Antiques Show Management: Diane Wendy

Diane Wendy is the founder of Wendy Management, a company that puts on about thirty antiques shows a year. She started the business in 1968, when her daughter Meg was twelve. Meg, now married and the mother of two little boys, joined the business in 1979, and mother and daughter today run one of the most profitable and highly respected antiques show management companies in the field.

How did all this come about? Let Diane tell you herself: "I loved my family, but being a housewife at home with a baby all day ... that just wasn't for me and I became depressed. A wise friend gave me a three-word prescription: 'Get a job.' So I did."

Diane went to work as a gofer, or "girl Friday" as it was called back in those pre-feminist days, for an antiques management company. She had always loved and collected antiques, so it was a natural. Within a few years, she was running the company, and when the boss decided to retire, she asked to buy it.

"Can you imagine?" she said. "He knew I had the capability to handle the business and the money to buy it, but he wouldn't sell it to a woman without my husband's cosignatures on all the papers!"

Diane loved the business and it flourished. But hearkening back to the greater complexity of a woman's life and priorities, Diane felt the need to be a full-time motherly presence when Meg became a teenager in the wild 1970s, so she moved the company offices into her home, where it still operates today. When Meg graduated from college, she went to work selling for IBM. After two years of working her way up in the commercial world, she asked her mother if she could work with her. Having grown up with the business right at home, Meg knew the field well and was able to slide right in.

"You have to love and understand antiques," said both Diane and Meg.

Why is it imperative that you must be knowledgeable about antiques? After all, you don't sell them, you just sell space to those who do. However, in order to run a show that brings in repeat traffic, you must carefully evaluate the exhibitors to insure that their merchandise is of authentically high caliber to attract the trust of collectors. Once these addicts—and serious antique collectors are that—learn that they can depend on finding good buys and authentically valuable pieces at your shows, they will keep coming and attendance will increase. Wendy Management shows have developed a tremendous number of faithful followers who come back year after year, and even travel to nearby cities to attend.

Running shows involves renting a large space (like an armory), dividing it into booths which are rented to concessionaires, and publicizing the show to bring in the buying public who pay to attend. The booth rentals cover your expenses; the gate fees are your profit.

Diane, Meg, and I were sitting on the screened porch overlooking the pool in the lovely antique-filled Wendy home, adjacent to the room which functions as the office of Wendy Management. Suddenly I heard noises downstairs and Diane smiled. "That's our mailroom in the basement. We send out 100,000 mailing pieces to announce our shows to our own mailing list of steady customers. It's all done right here, by my former housekeeper."

She explained that when her housekeeper of twenty-two years began to find housework difficult, Diane put her to work doing what is known in the direct mail trade as "mail fulfillment," which means putting addresses and postage on printed mailers, bundling them in zip codes and bringing the packages to the post office. It also means "cleaning" the mailing list by correcting addresses as customers move. Much of this is done by computer.

As we chatted and sipped coffee, Meg kept springing up to take phone calls from antique dealers who wanted to rent space in upcoming Wendy shows.

"Right now, our next eighteen shows are completely booked," she said with a proud smile.

Meg's job, among others, is to screen new applicants. She will draw a Dun & Bradstreet report and ask for photographs of their merchandise. Then both Diane and Meg will evaluate the pieces in order to insure their quality and authenticity.

"First-time exhibitors need guidance," said Diane. "I tell them they may not make much on their initial show, but if the merchandise is well-chosen and displayed, their sales should build. I suggest they give it three tries. If they don't make money by the third show, then they shouldn't be in the business."

Running a successful show management business imposes many demands. It means being at every show, which usually lasts three days. You must be on the floor, watching the gate and supervising the entire exhibit, dealing with potential crises and the demands and needs of exhibitors. The show manager must lay out the show wisely, by grouping suitable booths in specific locations, to make it easy for attendees to find their specific collectibles. The overall appearance, too, must be artistic—not tacky—and the displays must be tasteful. An eating area must be set up so that food is available both to visitors and exhibitors. To have a successful show, management must anticipate and provide for the needs of everyone.

Meg, who lives in a house directly across the street, excused herself to run over to look in on her baby, who was with a nanny but had a slight fever; she was back in ten minutes. After she acknowledged my comment about the great convenience of living nearby, I turned to Diane and asked how she enjoyed the arrangement that permitted her the privilege and pleasure of being able to witness and participate in the growing up of her grandchildren. Diane smiled broadly.

"It's absolutely wonderful."

Independent Antique Dealer: Selma Anderson

Selma Anderson of Keene, New Hampshire, has always been a lover and avid collector of nineteenth century silver.

"I grew up with it. It was a passion in our family."

Like all truly committed collectors, she is forever seeking out pieces at flea markets, auctions, and antiques shows. One of her greatest pleasures is discussing her collection with other enthusiasts, and educating and maybe turning on neophytes to the joys of collecting. This is an obsession that usually costs money, but Selma figured out a way to have it *make money* for her.

"I used to go to local flea markets," she said, "and one day I just thought 'I could do that.'" So she rented a booth in the next available show and found not only that she enjoyed it, but it was profitable.

Ten years later, the Anderson Gallery of Keene, New Hampshire, is an established antique dealership that exhibits at the Wendy Shows and others as far away as Georgia, Michigan, and Kentucky. Selma has created a loyal clientele that she circularizes constantly. She works out of her home where she sees buyers by appointment, although her principal business is conducted at antiques shows and by mail order to established customers.

Trust is a basic precept in the antiques business. The customer must trust the dealer's knowledgeable representations of the value and provenance of each piece, and the dealer has to trust the customer's honesty. This takes time and the building of relationships with customers becomes the business's most valuable asset.

"I get calls from customers all the time asking me to choose and ship wedding gifts for them. I send them two or three often quite expensive pieces to choose from, with full confidence that they'll return the rejected ones with a check for the accepted one. Many times they just ask me to choose and ship the gift directly to the bride and send me a check without ever even seeing what they bought."

What makes this business so ideal for women is the flexibility it offers for controlling growth along with the changes in family demands. While Selma's children were small, she confined her participation to local shows. And when she did travel, she was fortunate to have a husband whose local floral business kept him near home and available, plus nearby willing grandparents. Now that her children are grown and on their own, Selma does a great deal of traveling.

"I love the business. I enjoy educating my customers about silver." Knowledge instills interest, interest develops into enthusiasm, and enthusiasm creates collectors. Selma finds it fiscally rewarding and emotionally gratifying to help people learn how to derive pleasure from the appreciation of the beauty, artistry, and workmanship of early artisans.

Selma Anderson's entrepreneurial drive was fueled by the realization that she could convert her collecting hobby into a going business with minimal risk. She began with a $25,000 inventory, "But I always knew I could sell everything at auction if the business didn't work out."

This is a business that offers true independence. There is no overhead, there are no employees. The only expenses are travel, insurance, costs of merchandise movers, rentals of booths and showcases, and frequent mailings to clients. It offers the wonderful feature of total time flexibility; Selma selects the shows in which to participate, so that she can control her own life schedule and enjoy the pleasures of free time. Many antique dealers open shops which they either close when they go to shows, or leave in charge of trusted temporary employees or partners, but Selma prefers the non-shop route. She is not tied down to a 9-to-5 regimen. As an independent antique dealer, she is a one-person business who is responsible to and for no one but herself.

Creating Unique Recipes: Nancy Battista DeStefano

Say you are a great cook, but not the kind who must slavishly replicate cookbook directions; you read recipes for guidance and then go off to create your own version.

If tarragon and mustard go well on roast chicken, you try them in chicken salad. If bananas-and-sour-cream was a childhood favorite, why not extend the concept to a sophisticated dinner party dessert by mixing honey with the cream and pouring it over coconut-covered honeydew balls? By now you may have created one special dish that everyone adores, like a marvelous sauce that you bottle and give to friends. Maybe you should think of *selling* the stuff instead of giving it away.

Nancy Battista DiStefano's father used to bring home bushels of tomatoes every summer, which his wife and daughters peeled, boiled, and put up in Mason jars. Come winter, these canned tomatoes would be the base of pasta sauce made by adding herbs and spices. Nancy was always a divergent thinker in the kitchen, and one day she asked: "Why can't we mix the herbs with the tomatoes when we jar? Then we have ready-made sauce all the time."

The family told her this was not traditional and couldn't be done. So she did it herself and created a recipe which she named *pomodoro fresca*, which is Italian for "fresh tomatoes." Soon, the family basement was filled with shelves of Nancy's sauce. Today, she is the head of a flourishing business called Pomodoro Fresca Foods, Inc. that has been written up in the *New York Times* and her sauce has been awarded the coveted "Outstanding New Product of the Year" award from the National Association for the Specialty Store Trade.

Nancy's impetus to go into business came about when her husband of just a few years, and the father of her two-year old son, announced he wanted out of their marriage. Stunned and heartbroken she asked: "Don't you love me any more?"

His answer was a request to drive him to the train station. The ego-shattering effect of this abandonment compounded with the need to support her child transformed this slim, lovely young woman into a driving entrepreneur.

It all started with her job as a technician for a design company in New York, a business that required frequent use of caterers to provide food for meetings. Looking for another source of income, Nancy offered to cater these lunches for less than they were paying, and they agreed to give her a shot. Armed with her *pomodoro* sauce and a massive dose of chutzpah, she prepared an "Italian Peasant Fare" meal in which everything was in some way mixed or covered with a variation of her sauce. Success was instantaneous; they loved it, and she began to cater all their meetings. Some of the guests asked her to cater for their companies, and soon she had business cards, and a growing catering sideline. People were constantly asking to buy the sauce. Her big break came when a hit Swedish rock group named China asked her to take on the job of supplying their meals every night. They adored her *pomodoro fresca* and she put it on everything. For one year, she worked a full day at the design company (she didn't yet have the confidence or cash to quit), dashed home to cook, and drove back into New York City with the food and her little son Daniel.

"I knew I couldn't keep this pace up forever. People told me I should sell my sauce. But I didn't have any money."

By the end of the year, she had made enough money to risk going into business producing Pomodoro Fresca. Her only problem was—how?

First, she needed a production facility larger than her kitchen. Her brother had some unused space in back of his ice cream store, which became her first "factory." She worked there for endless hours, with a crew of local women to produce the sauce, and then went around from store to store selling it. The big break came when one of her brother's ice cream cone customers got her an introduction to the Food Emporium, a chain of upscale supermarkets. Equipped with jars bearing mock-up labels, and absolutely no idea of how the grocery business works, she made her presentation to the executives. After finishing his sample, one of the executives asked, "What makes you think our customers will like this sauce?"

She looked pointedly as his wiped-clean second plate. "You did, didn't you?"

She walked out with a trial order for forty cases, plus specific instructions about their requirements for proper processing, labeling, and packaging.

Nancy then took a six-hour drive to Geneva, New York, to the Cornell University Cooperative Extension Program of the Department of Agriculture, for instruction on food processing procedures. She then went back to her brother's and transformed the back of his ice cream parlor into a legal, proper food manufacturing facility. They—that means the entire family—were now ready to produce the first major food store order.

"It took us from 6:00 in the morning till midnight to produce forty cases of sauce. We all worked at different shifts, me, my brother and sisters, my mother, my father."

The unique quality of Pomodoro Fresca is that it is made only of fresh tomatoes that are actually cooked in the jars. Nancy knew if she were to become a real pasta sauce production company, she couldn't continue to buy her tomatoes in small quantities at retail prices from the supermarket. She had to find produce wholesalers.

The Hunts Point Wholesale Food Market, in the toughest South Bronx section of New York, is not recommended for midnight visits by a pretty young woman with a baby, and a mother carrying a big cash-filled pocketbook.

"The first time we went there," said Nancy, "we were scared to death. It's only open at night, and believe me, there were some tough looking guys around. One night we saw a man get shot, another night there was a stabbing. But I kept coming. I needed tomatoes and no one was going to stop me."

You'd think the men might feel sorry for, maybe a bit protective of, this young, pretty, inexperienced, hardworking mother who would usually have her small son in tow. Instead, they took advantage of her naivete and tried to cheat her whenever possible. She learned to mark the cartons of high quality tomatoes she had paid for to prevent getting delivery of inferior substitutes. She learned to become a tough negotiator and to fight for the lowest possible prices.

The sauce was selling well and production was becoming a problem. Then she met a businessman who was looking for someone to share his new plant for making kosher food entrees. Impressed with Nancy's potential, he offered to invest $100,000 in Pomodoro Fresca Foods, Inc. in return for 45 percent interest in the company, and to lease her half the space in his building.

Today, Pomodoro has distributors in California, Colorado,

Illinois, Massachusetts, Maryland, and Florida, and is acquiring more distributors constantly. Nancy's business day is now a far cry from those hectic eighteen-hour grinds. She works normal hours and is able to schedule her time to be able to pick up Daniel from school. Our interview took place in her private office in a modern building in Millburn, New Jersey. We walked into the plant where she checked over operations with her sister and mother, who are in charge of manufacturing in the spotless factory that boasts eight-foot-tall three hundred-gallon kettles and a crew of women workers. Her lawyer, accountant, and supervisors, too, are all women.

"When I walk around the plant and see what we accomplished here, I still get butterflies in my stomach!" She told me that she was lucky enough to get a number of breaks. As I pointed out to her, luck had little to do with it. Persistence, imagination, and her refusal to accept failure, based on a deep belief in her product and herself, are what made her enterprise succeed.

It all started with a recipe. The Sara Lee Company started in a woman's kitchen, as did Pepperidge Farms bakeries. Many women enjoy getting raves from friends and family about their cooking specialties, but it is the entrepreneurial woman, like Nancy Battista DiStefano, who starts to wonder "Why give it away when I can sell it?" and then has the guts and drive to build it into a business.

Opening an Inn and Restaurant: Mim Perle

Mim Perle started an enterprise at age fifty that made her and her husband millionaires, brought their family together, and gave their children a substantial business and a secure future. This is the kind of fulfillment-of-a-dream story that might not make it into a CBS TV Movie-of-the-Week, but will surely make you smile and feel good.

East Hampton, New York, is the posh 'n' arty second-home site for the rich and famous, as well as for those who flock there in order to wow the folks at home with a litany of celebrities spotted at the local supermarket. As you come into one of the loveliest Main Streets in America, bordered on both sides by ancient trees and beautifully maintained seventeenth and eighteenth century buildings, you will see a simple, elegant white house with the small sign "1770." In the back is a tranquil garden, and inside are lovingly furnished rooms filled with authentic antiques and a restaurant serving the finest food in the area.

This is the establishment run by the Perle family. Mim and Sid Perle are the chief executive officers, daughter Wendy is the pastry chef, son-in-law Burton Van Heusen helps run the place, son Adam handles the bar, and Adam's wife Joy manages the front desk. It is one of the most elegant and sought-after hostelries in the area. The dining room seats forty and there are two seatings a night from Thursday to Sunday, and reservations are prized. The seven guest rooms, furnished with antique canopied beds and modern, beautifully appointed bathrooms, rent for $100 to $195 a night, including a breakfast of hot homemade scones and jam.

"I always loved to cook," said Mim. We were sitting in the sunny, huge living room of the twenty-room mansion that she and Sid bought in 1984. "I remember basting a leg of lamb for my mother when I was nine years old. I grew up cooking. I was an art major in college but when I got married and we moved to Franklin Square in Long Island, I started cooking for everyone. My professional career really began when a friend asked me to cook for her son's bar mitzvah. She couldn't afford a caterer, so I did it." She smiled as she recalled her nervousness. "There were fifty-three guests. My friend paid for the food . . . and I got the grand total of $35 for my labors." One day, another friend who was a travel agent phoned her. "Mim, there's a special tour that just came in. Round-trip to Paris and eight weeks training at the Cordon Bleu. I just signed you up."

"I was scared," said Mim. "I had never even been away from home before."

With the cooperation of her husband and two teenaged children, she went off and learned her craft in the most prestigious cooking school in the world. On her return, she came across a small, empty shop in town and decided to open her own cooking school. She also prepared foods, such as hors d'oeuvres and cakes, which she sold to Bloomingdale's and all the gourmet food stores throughout the area. She did this for thirteen years. Then one day she and Sid took a trip to the Amish country in Lancaster, Pennsylvania, and Mim had one of those epiphanies that change lives.

"When I saw those big houses with three generations living together—parents, children, grandparents—it seemed so right and wonderful, the way life once was but no longer is."

Son Adam was out of college and uncertain about what to do. Daughter Wendy, who had worked in restaurants while going through college, was talking about marrying a young artist and they were unsettled. Sid had a men's clothing store in New York City's Pennsylvania Station, which was profitable but joyless.

"When I broached the idea of buying an inn and restaurant where we would live and work together, all of us loved the idea, but our accountant advised against it. 'You can't count on more than 85 percent capacity in the summer, and nothing in the winter. At $45 a room, you'll never make it.' I thought that was ridiculous. We'll make it, and if we don't we can always go back to making a living the way we used to."

In any life-changing action, timing is the vital factor. Mim intuitively recognized that now was the right time. They scoured the area for old houses for sale, and heard that the 1770 house in East Hampton was up for auction. It was in deplorable shape; the original building, erected in 1650, had additions in 1890 but little had been done since.

"We bought it for $125,000." she said simply. "Sid sold his share of the business to his partner and we sold our house in Great Neck. Everybody told us we were crazy. Sid and I were fifty years old. 'What kind of time is this to start a new business?' But to me it wasn't just a new business, it was a new life for all of us.

"We worked like people obsessed. We tore off wallpaper, we ripped tiles off the walls."

Everyone worked, including Sid's and Mim's sisters. Thanks to the fact that Sid had been an avid antique collector for many years, they had almost enough authentic pieces and ornaments, including his marvelous old clock collection, to fill the rooms. For three months, while the place was being rebuilt, they accumulated more furniture and decorative objects from auctions and estate sales all over Long Island.

"We opened on Labor Day 1977—and were filled to capacity from the first night."

Unfortunately, they missed the summer season but since the building was heated and there were fireplaces in almost every room, they were able to remain open all winter. Although East Hampton is basically a summer resort, there are enough permanent residents in the surrounding villages as well as year-round weekenders to provide plenty of business.

"1770" is one of the most successful inns and restaurants in East Hampton, and that's really saying something in a town frequented and inhabited by the sophisticates of the film, theatre, art, and publishing worlds. When Steven Spielberg married Kate Capshaw in East Hampton, his family stayed at the Inn and Mim provided a special luncheon for the wedding guests, among them Barbra Streisand.

I went to "1770" for dinner on a Saturday night at the height of the season and was greeted by a smiling, urbane Sid, who obviously reveled in his role as host. He handled the crush of guests with charm and skill, as though he was born to the job. Mim came over to sit with me and I enjoyed the stares of diners who wondered who I was to rate a table visit from the owner and chef.

As befits founders of one of the finest hostelries in town, Mim and Sid Perle enjoy near-celebrity status in East Hampton. Their pictures have appeared in numerous newspaper and magazine stories, along with commendatory stories about the inn and restaurant.

Wendy, now married to the artist, Burt Van Heusen, lives with him and their two young daughters in a nearby house. Adam and his new bride recently bought a home in the area. Two years ago, Mim and Sid gave the restaurant to their children. They retain the property and inn facilities, plus their home.

"Until 1984," Mim told me, "we lived on the inn's third floor. I felt like Cinderella. We decided it was time to get our own place, so I asked the real estate broker to find us a little house nearby."

I looked around at the magnificent mansion that took up a full half-block, with a one-half acre topiary garden in back and laughed. "This is the 'little house'?"

"We thought the agent was out of his mind, too," said Mim. "But he explained that the owner was eager to sell and the price was a bargain. We fell in love with it, of course, but how could we afford it? Then we learned that East Hampton law allows you to rent out up to one-third of a house provided it's your primary residence. I saw that three of the bedrooms were ideally situated for guests without affecting our privacy. We would just run it as sort of an extension of '1770'. So we bought it."

Today, the Perles live in baronial splendor in a million-dollar mansion on Main Street, just a few blocks away from their inn. As Mim told me, the house, with the Mercedes in the driveway, represents to Sid the epitome of his, or in fact any man's, ambitions.

They have a secure income, substantial property, and a highly profitable business. They have the great parental pleasure of being able to provide a solid business and good lives for their children and grandchildren, as well as the joy of having all of them around, living and working together.

And it all started with a woman who had the imagination to take her talent and convert it into a vehicle that would make a better life for her family. It succeeded because she had the courage to take risks and the insight to bring her husband and children into the project, so that it became the satisfying fulfillment of all their dreams.

Estate and Tag Sale Management: Carol Mencher

What would you do if your family gave you the job of selling the contents of your recently deceased grandmother's home, and you later learned that the so-called reliable dealer who purchased everything took advantage of your inexperience and bereavement, and gave you a fraction of what things were worth?

Carol Mencher's reaction was anger. She determined to do something to protect other people from such unscrupulous dealers by creating a better alternative for disposing of an entire home. She started a business, now known throughout the New York metropolitan area, New Jersey, and Connecticut as Treasure Hunters Estates and Tag Sales, Inc. The time was exactly right for such an enterprise, and her company actually became the basis of a new small industry that filled an important need.

Until seventy-five years ago, it was customary for people to stay in one house throughout their lives but by the end of the 1940s, the old "family homestead" had become strictly a thing of the past. Newlyweds now buy a "first house," the real estate pages' term denoting a modest home that the couple expect to trade up from as soon as their fortunes improve. And when they do, they'll want to sell off their simple starter furniture in order to buy more impressive pieces befitting the new abode, so they'll usually run a garage sale to dump the junk. Thirty years later, when their children are grown and out on their own, do they stay in the big house and sit rocking on the porch waiting for the kids to visit? Are you kidding? They sell the place and are off to a condo in Florida. Now they have a lifetime's accumulation of costly possessions to get rid of because everybody knows you can have only white formica and lucite furniture in the Sunbelt. The furnishings of their large house are now too extensive and valuable to dispose of in a dinky garage sale. It's time to call in the experts—a tag sale management company.

"When we started the business," said Carol, "tag sales didn't exist. Garage sales are when you sell an accumulation of things; tag sales are when you sell an entire house."

Carol had married young, and by twenty had two daughters. Within a few years, she began to realize that the marriage would not last. "I had never worked, but I knew I had to have a career plan for my future."

She had an art history background, which enabled her to get a job with a gallery owned by a woman who ran art auctions for various charities. Carol became the liaison to these organizations.

One day, the gallery owner had to go through the onerous task of disposing of her mother's life belongings. Carol commiserated with her about the hassles involved. Wouldn't it be wonderful, she suggested, if there was an agent who could handle the entire job of evaluating the items and then sell them for the highest possible prices. Why not them? This might be something they could do over the summer, when gallery business was slow.

"You bring in one friend," said Carol's boss, "and I'll bring in one friend, and let's try it."

Thus a business and an industry was born.

Their first customers were women Carol had worked with in the various charity organizations. They were affluent, and of an age where they might be moving to smaller homes, apartments, or Florida condos. They knew and trusted Carol, and were delighted to find someone who would take over the enormous task of selling the contents of an entire home. The mental as well as physical demands are overwhelming for a single individual.

"We do everything," said Carol. "We appraise, price, and tag every single object. We organize each room. We bring in our staff of reliable people. And, most important, we bring in the right customers by advertising to our special mailing list of over two thousand selected buyers, who come to all our sales because they know they will be seeing objects of worth that are fairly priced."

Tag sale attendees are a special breed. They get hooked almost to the point of addiction. The attraction is twofold: it touches the yenta in us by affording a chance to peek into other people's homes and lifestyles, and it appeals to our bargain-hunting instincts. Since these are usually the homes of fairly well-to-do people, it gives less-fortunates the immense satisfaction of "tsk-tsking" at the deplorable state of the house (and no place looks more desolate than a home with drapeless windows, walls that have been stripped of paintings leaving white patches, and furniture piled in the middle of each room), and the gratifying opportunity to comment "Hmmph, the way some people live!"

Micheline and Bernadette, two Frenchwomen with whom I play tennis regularly, leave our Friday morning game every week to head for a tag sale. It's an adventure and, in a sense, a nostalgia trip. I accompanied them to a tag sale where, with great joy, I fell upon an insert dish for a six-piece hors d'oeuvre server I had bought in my newlywed days and had not been able to use for years after breaking one of the dishes. Where else could I have found replacement parts for something bought so long ago? It was like a lovely voyage down memory lane. "I always liked old things," said Carol, "but that's not enough. You have to be knowledgeable in order to appraise every item."

The four partners who began Treasure Hunters each had a different area of expertise. "No one person can know everything," continued Carol. "I started to take every course offered, and still do. I have learned about bric-a-brac, silver, porcelain, oriental rugs, old books. You can't expect to be an expert in every field, so you have specialists you can call on. But you must be knowledgeable enough to recognize something good."

She told me that she had made some major finds, such as a drawing for which the seller wanted only $200 because she hated it. It turned out to be a Max Beckmann and Carol sold it for a bit more—$20,000. Treasure Hunters runs an average of forty sales a year, and they derive their income from the 20 to 25 percent commission earned on whatever they sell. When the business first started, they could not afford to be too selective and took on every home that was offered. Today, a home has to be able to produce at least $6,000 in sales merely to cover expenses.

Carol Mencher had the foresight to see that this was a particularly ideal business for women because the volume of activity can be adjusted to the demands of various stages of life. When her children were young, she took on just the number of projects she could comfortably handle. Also, since the major activity—the actual sale—occurs on weekends when people are not at work, she was able to find a family member—a grandparent or even friend or neighbor—to look after the kids. When the children got a bit older, she started taking them with her. Now her daughters are grown, with their own careers, but they often help their mother at tag sales.

This business is particularly suited for multiple ownership. For one thing, partners bring in varied areas of expertise. They also permit a division of labor to dovetail with everyone's priorities. The partner with school-age children can handle the appraisals of homes of potential clients which is normally done on weekdays, and the partner with the weekend-golfer husband can run the sales on Saturday and Sunday.

"After seventeen years, I still find this business as challenging and exciting as ever. This weekend, we're running two sales—one is a contemporary house, one is a very traditional one. It's always something different; that's what makes this business so interesting," said Carol enthusiastically. "I find myself sometimes working seven days a week, but that's my choice. I love the work. You meet all kinds of people and you get to see all kinds of lifestyles, and you never know what the next day will bring."

Landscape Design and Gardening: Beverly Gussoff

Beverly Gussoff always loved gardening. She was way past picking up plants at supermarkets and garden centers, but had become a habitue of nurseries where she revelled in seeing new specimens and rare plantings. She took adult education gardening courses and those offered by the local botanical gardens. Some people flip first in the Sunday paper to the crossword puzzle; she would go to the gardening columns. Some women spend extravagantly on furs; she spent money on her garden. Some women just sit back and take pride in the fact that they had created what became a neighborhood showplace. That's just what Beverly Gussoff did until special situations made her sit up and decide to convert her hobby into a business.

When Beverly moved into a new house with her husband and two small sons, the place had the spotty and sparse landscaped look so favored by frugal builders. She knew something needed doing, but didn't know quite what and how to do it. So she took a course in gardening at the local botanical gardens and discovered a new passion. She started buying and planting, and found an eager helper in the form of her seven-year-old son Michael. Together, they built a rock garden, and then a woodland garden that bordered the brook in back of the house.

As the years passed, she and Michael were creating more and more ambitious projects for their now exquisitely landscaped grounds. He loved to work there after school, and she would come home from her job and head for the garden.

"I found I was spending an average of $5,000 a year on the garden," said Beverly. "I kept redesigning, creating new gardens, and looking for unusual specimens."

More years passed. By now, son Jeffrey was a lawyer and the father of a baby daughter. Michael had graduated from Marquette University and was now national sales and marketing manager for a scientific equipment company. But gardening was still a consuming hobby, and he found time to work with his mother on their gardening, which had now expanded to creating gardens as favors for friends and relatives who admired their work.

"I spent hours in nurseries looking for just the right shrub for a particular spot in my friend's garden," said Beverly. It was fun, and she enjoyed every minute of it. Then two things happened that brought about one of those critical turning points that force you to evaluate life choices and make the risk-taking decision that will inevitably alter your future.

First, Beverly's job changed and she was informed that she would soon have to commute to another city. Second, she accidentally learned how to buy gardening materials and plants wholesale rather than at the more costly retail price.

When chatting with the owner of the garden center where she had been spending thousands of dollars, she noticed an advertisement for an upcoming gardening trade show in Valley Forge, Pennsylvania. Eager to see a greater range of exotic plants, she asked him for details only to be told firmly that this show was strictly for the trade and she could not be admitted without a business card. When she mentioned her disappointment to Michael, he went to the local print shop and had business cards printed for "Primrose Landscape Design Company," a name they came up with quickly since their house was on Primrose Avenue. Being a seasoned businessman, Michael knew that "strictly for the trade" prohibitions are usually mythical and almost impossible to enforce. Anyone with a business card is admitted, since exhibitors are anxious to move merchandise and it's the size of the order that determines their acceptance of a customer. If you buy enough, they will be happy to sell and ship as long as you pay in advance. Beverly and Michael attended the show and were enthralled.

"I saw grafted hemlocks, weeping Norway spruces, and red pines," said Beverly. "It was awesome."

This was the catalyst that made her turn her beloved hobby into a business. Coincidentally, Michael was becoming disenchanted with the corporate world, and wanted to do something entrepreneurial. The timing was right.

"We pooled our money, $50,000," she said, "which we invested in equipment and marketing."

They set up offices in the playroom and basement of the Gussoff house, bought a fax, computer, designing table, desks, and filing cabinet. Beverly had the unique advantage of having a son and partner with marketing savvy. Michael knew the importance of projecting professionalism in a field where lawn-mowing maintenance men who can't spell the word "horticulture" touted themselves as landscapers. Since they were selling esthetics, their image had to reflect style and taste. Their logo, a pink-and-green Primrose, was featured on letterheads, business cards, and on the sides of their white van. They and their workers also wore T-shirts and sweatshirts imprinted with the logo.

At the beginning, they both held on to their day jobs and ran the business after work. Investing your money is one thing, but giving up your livelihood is a risk that should be postponed as long as possible.

"We made our plans in the fall of 1986 and in the spring of 1987, we had our first client. A couple wanted their house landscaped so that they could sell it faster. When we finished that job—and incidentally, the landscaping looked so beautiful that they decided to stay in the house—we got three more clients in the neighborhood."

Like any new business, it took a year to really get going and both of them worked day and night. By the second year, they went into the black; the company was producing enough income for both of them to give up their jobs and give it their full-time attention.

Beverly does the design, and Michael handles the running and administration of the business. In Primrose's first four years of operation, the company showed a growth of 200 percent; even last year, during what most businesses regarded as a slow recession period, the increase was almost 130 percent. Assignments run from a 25 × 8 ft. border to a complete landscaping program costing from $2,000 to $10,000. One of the advantages of their business is that people who spend large sums on landscaping are anxious to protect their investments and usually contract for year-round maintenance. As a result, ninety-nine percent of their landscaping installations produce a steady income stream for the company.

As Beverly showed me proudly around her own gardens, I was struck by the beauty and sense of serenity she had created. Along the side of the house is a small nursery of shrubs and flowers awaiting planting in customers' gardens. I noticed a workman wearing a Primrose T-shirt and asked how and where they found competent labor to do the digging and heavy work.

"Every one of our men came to us through recommendation. The original crew were friends of our masonry contractor's foreman. We figured he would know reliable, hard-working men— men like himself. And he did. One brought the other, which is good since people who are friends work better together."

Although Beverly was not an experienced entrepreneur, she instinctively understood the value of a contented corps of employees. "We've developed a core group of loyal workers," she said. "They know we'll treat them fairly," which is not all that usual in a business that hires day laborers on a when-needed basis. "We take care of them—pick them up and take them home. We always bring them breakfast, and hot and cold drinks during the day."

Primrose Landscape has a regular direct mail program, but recommendation and word-of-mouth is their most effective business builder. They recently contracted for landscaping and maintenance at a sizable townhouse development, a job they won by creative selling.

"They asked us to submit a proposal with elaborate designs. But we knew the co-op board would never be able to envision the installation from black-and-white drawings," said Beverly. "So we organized a three-vehicle caravan and took them to view some of the houses we did in the area. They loved the looks of the places, but what really convinced them was when the homeowners came out and greeted me with hugs and kisses. There's nothing more impressive than satisfied customers."

Today Beverly Gussoff is a very contented woman. She marvels at the fact that she can make money pursuing her beloved hobby. She has the pleasure of being instrumental in her son's escape from a stressful suit-and-tie corporate existence into the casual jeans-and-shirt world of the suburban executive, as well as helping him build a solid, profitable business for his future. Every day, her husband goes off happily to his own business, and she and Michael stay home to work in their business. It's an everybody-wins situation.

Publishing a Newspaper: Merna Popper

To say that anyone who writes well should become the publisher of a newspaper would be like suggesting that anyone adept at removing splinters should become a brain surgeon.

It ain't that easy. But Merna Popper did it.

Today she is the publisher of *Women's News*, a monthly newspaper that covers Westchester County, an affluent suburb of New York City. Twelve years ago, Merna was a homemaker with a fourteen-year-old daughter, a seventeen-year-old-son, and a husband whose frequent business forays were making Merna feel like she had a third child. The financial insecurity of the family, coupled with her own need to use her capabilities, caused her to search for an income-producing outlet for her energy.

"I studied art history at Sarah Lawrence," she said, "so I figured I ought to work in the art field."

She picked up a few assignments writing reviews of art exhibits and discovered a new truth about herself: she enjoyed the writing part more than the art.

One evening, at a dinner party, she met a woman who had been a journalist and Merna mentioned that she was seeking a coauthor for a book she was planning to do about women of achievement; a collaboration was formed instantly.

"We began to research and write," said Merna.

After completing about four chapters, they became interested in the exciting new phenomenon of women emerging into positions of power and decided that this movement could be the basis of more than a one-time book. Why not an ongoing publication like a newspaper?

They named it *Women's News*: a monthly newspaper for women, by women. Like most women's start-up enterprises, it all began on the dining room table. Like most partnerships, each brought a specific strength to the project.

"My partner had the journalistic know-how and I had the vision," said Merna with a smile.

As I sat in her office and watched her field phone calls, handle employee interruptions, and answer my questions—all without missing a beat or losing her cool—it was apparent that she also has the strong, decisive mentality of a successful executive.

As *Women's News* got bigger, the dining room table got smaller. A sympathetic friend offered them the use of her summer home, and once a month the copublishers would leave their families and spend one week putting out the paper. They both wrote articles, and Merna designed the layout of each page. After a year of this procedure, they decided to bring the work home and moved to Merna's basement.

They used their own money to start the paper, and depended upon advertising to help keep it afloat. As the publication became better known, more and more advertisers came in and they hit the breakeven point. However, growth requires more equipment, more expense, and reinvestment of capital. It now came time to lease a copier, enlarger, and reproducing machine, which required the partners to sign a lease for $7,000. Since they were not yet profitable, the leasing company required personal signatures for the indebtedness. At that point, Merna's partner balked; she wanted out. Not only was she loathe to incur any risk, but she had become increasingly disillusioned with the fact that the paper had been all work and no pay. A basic rule of any new business is that, at the outset, all income must be plowed back into the enterprise to keep it going and growing. For as long as it takes the business to go into the black and produce a healthy profit, salaries are paid to employees, but never to owners.

Merna bought out her partner and was now the sole publisher. "I alone signed for the $7,000." she said.

She believed in *Women's News*. She also believed in herself and was willing to take risks. As the newspaper expanded and added pages, production activities in Merna's basement began to draw the ire of neighbors and she could no longer run the paper from home. By this time, her marriage was on its way out and her children were grown and off on their own: it was the moment to make a definitive move. Unlike homemakers who often are destroyed by divorce and a totally empty nest, Merna had the business to fill her life and help maintain her self-esteem and sanity through what could have been a devastating period.

In February 1990, eight years after its first issue, *Women's News* moved into its own one-story building in Harrison, New York. Today, *Women's News* distributes two regional monthly editions throughout the county of Westchester, New York to two hundred fifty thousand readers. The publication has twelve full-time employees, plus a cadre of freelance writers and a staff of commissioned salespeople who fill the pages with local as well as national ads. It is a newsy, entertaining, and highly informative publication filled with columns and items about women, for women. Recently, it sponsored a symposium with Elizabeth Dole speaking on the topic of "Why shouldn't a woman be more like a woman?" that drew thousands in attendance. As publisher of a twelve-year-old newspaper, Merna is a highly respected power in the community. An attractive blonde dynamo, she is a popular member of the high-level movers and shakers of the county. She has her own one-hour show on a local radio station where she interviews people of both local and national prominence. Backed by the clout of a quarter-of-a-million readers, Merna is sought after by officials and politicians and has used that power to further the rise of women in commerce and government. There are many local women candidates who owe their judgeships or congressional seats to her support.

"Whenever we write an article about a woman executive, she either gets a raise or a promotion," said Merna.

When you enter the offices of *Women's News*, you see a hive of obviously well-directed activity. There are women walking about purposefully, women at desks; everyone looks busy and happy. Merna's small front office is piled with books and papers, and her guiding role as publisher is apparent as employees' heads constantly come peeking in the door with questions.

Like many women entrepreneurs, Merna started her business armed only with an idea and a willingness to take risks. Learning the business was strictly an on-the-job training process. Twelve years ago, before women were taken seriously as potential business builders, options were limited. Today, women entrepreneurs are much more fortunate because there are a myriad of guides and start-up aids available, including this book.

Public Relations: Carolyn B. Mandelker

"I started in 1987 at home with one client and three Ts," said Carolyn B. Mandelker. "A typewriter, a telephone, and a thesaurus."

Today she is the president and owner of an active, highly successful firm, Harrison Edwards, Inc. With three employees and a roster of clients for whom she does national and international public relations, Carol's company has gross sales in the healthy six figures.

When I asked Carol how the business came into being, she used the words I have heard from many women who built successful businesses: "It just sort of evolved." But there's always a beginning, when a sudden catalyst crystalizes ideas that have been floating around in your mind. For Carolyn, it was a casual Christmas party suggestion by a woman who was impressed with her very effective public relations activities for their children's school. She recommended that Carolyn make a pitch for the PR account of her husband's company because he was disenchanted with his current agency.

The timing was right. She had been thinking of starting a PR business. The physical facility already existed; when she and her husband moved with their two small sons into their house in Katonah, New York, they built an office set-up for her. When she lived in New York City, Carolyn had worked on political campaigns, including Mayor Ed Koch's. Now a resident of the suburbs with two young boys, she offered her talents to local organizations and began to do PR work for the school board, environmental board, the community hospital, and the Democratic party. She wrote news stories and placed them in newspapers and magazines, handled the promotion for benefits, and wrote newsletters.

When the opportunity arose to go professional, Carolyn spoke to PR agencies she knew to learn what was involved in running this sort of business. Public relations is the process of conveying a client's image and message to specific groups. The PR representative tries to get the client's activities and achievements into the news, by working with all the media to get and keep them interested in the client and by writing and placing stories in print and on TV and radio. It's a skill that requires writing ability, a talent for developing relationships with editors and journalists, and the imagination to recognize what, when, and how to promote.

Convinced that she could handle a business, Carolyn took up the invitation to call upon this potential "client" and made her presentation. "I got the account," she said proudly, "and I beat out a large New York City agency."

This took place in the winter of 1987. A few months later, a day-care center approached her to handle their public relations. By the spring, she had three clients.

"I started with just me and my basic office equipment. As time went on, I acquired more help in the form of employees and equipment. First came the copier, then the computer, then the fax," Carol explained.

As I mentioned earlier, the beauty of a service business is the low cost of launching it. Overhead is minimal, especially if you work at home. The only major expense is for labor, and if that's just you alone, your up-front risk is next to nothing. "My only initial outlay," she said, "was for stationery."

When I asked her how long it took for her to show a profit, she said: "Almost at once."

The company has been growing steadily and has won many awards for excellence. Her business operates effectively from home without in any way impinging on family life. Her husband and sons are gone all day; the boys go to school from 7:45 AM until 5 PM and her husband is a commuter. Thus she has no reason to incur the high overhead of an outside office.

I asked Carolyn how she came up with the company name of Harrison Edwards, Inc. "PR is perception and image," she said with a smile. "I wanted a name that sounded old and established. I might want to take in partners some day, and I dislike the way businesses keep changing their corporate names every time they add or drop a partner. Harrison Edwards, Inc. is a constant."

Marketing Home Furnishings: Helen Ballard

Helen Ballard started her first business when she was fifteen years old. She started her second one when she was twenty-eight. The first enterprise was a day-care center that had four employees and ran successfully for three summers; the second one is Ballard Designs of Atlanta, Georgia, a mail-order company that sells architectural pieces as furniture and, eleven years after it started, mails out six million catalogs a year and does an annual gross volume of twenty million dollars a year. There's a parallel in these start-up situations; they are both the result of the ability to recognize a need that could be translated into a business. Helen Ballard has that knack.

It came about because of Helen's hobby of searching out architectural bits and pieces and converting them into home furnishings. She was not a decorator, nor did she have any interior design training, but she apparently had a flair. Her apartment was filled with unique Helen Ballard designs that always brought comments and compliments. After friends encouraged her to enter *Metropolitan Home* magazine's contest for the most beautiful apartment, she won the southern division of the contest and her home was featured in the magazine. Then the calls started. Over five hundred people phoned to ask where they could buy a dining room table like hers, a glass-top supported by a base shaped like three dolphins, as well as other Ballard-made items.

"I got calls and calls from people asking where they could buy my things. I thought, why not from me? This might be a business." She discussed the idea with her parents, who were supportive.

"My father was a businessman, and he and my mother always encouraged my sister and me. They made us feel we could become whatever we wanted to be."

There were no gender limitations set up for the two girls. Helen's sister used to do science experiments in the closet; she was encouraged to become a doctor, not a nurse. Helen was always interested in commerce, and she was encouraged to become an executive, not a secretary.

"I started in the smallest way possible, at home with a type-writer. For start-up money, I sold my condo, moved into a rental apartment, and used the $15,000 profit. $10,000 went into the business, and I lived for a year on the $5,000. My first catalog was a shoestring operation. I did the photography, I wrote the copy, I did everything."

That first catalog was a simple two-page black-and-white brochure featuring ten items from her Atlanta condo. She ran ads in *Metropolitan Home* and *House Beautiful* for three months.

"The response was amazing," she said. "I made sales to nine out of ten people who called or wrote."

As the business grew, Helen found someone to make plaster casts of statuary for inside and outside the home. Pieces that usually cost $1,500 could now be had for $150. What started as a ten-product mail-order business has now become a large company marketing home furnishings and specializing in classical architectural reproductions. From the original two-page black and white catalog, the Ballard Design catalog has grown to over thirty full-color pages featuring over three hundred items of classical Greek and Roman columns and statues—that serve as table bases, lamps, bookends, and more—as well as linens and decorative accessories. The business that began with one woman sitting in her apartment at a typewriter has now become a seventy-two-employee organization operating out of a 50,000-square-foot building in Atlanta. In 1990, Helen Ballard was named "Georgia Entrepreneur of the Year" in the "Innovative Services" category. When she started the business, she worked seven days a week with time off to attend business classes on the basics of running a company. She read all the trade magazines; she tapped all the resources of the industry's trade association.

"I talked to everyone I knew in business. We had a group of women company owners who met for lunch whenever we could to sort of learn by comparing notes."

Today, Helen is a lot freer to take time off. Like every one of the women I interviewed, she has a sense of proprietary pride in the successful entity she has created. The business consumes a large portion of her life; like most involved entrepreneurs, Helen puts in about fifty to sixty hours a week. But at this point, this dedication is by choice, and as I listened to her describe the successful development of Ballard Designs, I could tell that she loves every minute of it.

Marketing Decorative Accessories: Agnes Rolnick

Agnes Rolnick of Houston, Texas, was happy—her daughter Susan was getting married. But when she and her daughter went off to the bridal registries to select china, glass, and silver patterns, they found that department store prices were astronomical. "Aggie" had grown up in New York City where discount stores abounded, so she assumed everything could be found elsewhere at lower prices. She searched, and learned that what was a given in New York was non-existent in Texas; everything was available strictly at retail list price in Houston.

"*Somebody* ought to start a discount place for these things around here," she thought. After the wedding was over and Agnes realized she needed something to occupy the rest of her life, she thought, "Why not me?"

Her father had been a furniture manufacturer. As an only child, Aggie spent a good deal of time in his plant and often traveled with him and her mother to trade shows. She had a strong artistic sense that developed into a feeling for design and quality. It seemed a natural to start a business selling decorative accessories.

Equipped with a powerful entrepreneurial urge and a large dose of chutzpah—plus a friend who had asked to join the enterprise—she and her partner flew off to a winter-frozen Europe in January 1984 on a buying trip to buy they knew not what from they knew not who.

"We just went off, cold turkey, and decided we'd find some sources who would export fine china, glass, and silver to us. The dollar was strong then, so we didn't need too deep a discount."

After much trudging around strange cities, asking all sorts of questions of all sorts of people, they came home with three suppliers, and they were in business. They now knew from whom to buy. Now to whom would they sell, and how?

The fastest, easiest way was to rent selling space at one of the charity-sponsored pre-Christmas sale shows that abound in Houston every year. Aggie and her partner set out their china and glassware, did a nice business, and began to participate in more and more shows. Total novices at first, they learned on the job and soon built up a customer base list of active buyers. As the business grew more demanding, Aggie's partner grew weary of the work and time required, so Aggie bought her out.

"At first my husband Len looked upon the business as just la-di-da ladies' work. You know, something to keep the little woman happy."

Aggie then created a Christmas gift catalog, which she mailed to her customer list. Orders poured in and she, her husband, and daughter packed, labeled, and mailed in the Rolnicks' living room—which became the warehouse and shipping department. Intermart, "Direct importers of fine European crystal, china, and silver at the best discount prices," had now become a business that the recently retired Len began to take seriously. He put the entire business on computer and took over the billing, inventory control, and all administrative chores, which totally freed Agnes to sell. She moved into Len's old office in a Houston office building and set up a showroom. By now, Intermart was mailing 80,000 catalogs. Susan worked with her and together they covered a dozen shows a year.

"The shows are good because customers tell me exactly what they want and I can detect trends as they happen."

For instance, as the national economy took a downswing, the average amount spent for wedding gifts began to drop. Aggie noticed that where before people looked for wedding gifts in the $80 to $100 category, more and more were now asking for $35 to $50 items. Her quick awareness of this change in buying habits enabled her to increase inventory of the newly-demanded lower-priced merchandise at the right time.

Today, Intermart is grossing in the millions of dollars. Aggie has given her husband a post-retirement occupation that keeps him stimulated and active, and has provided Susan, now the mother of two, with a job that she can coordinate easily with her family schedule.

From time to time, some of my students complain that there are no longer any frontiers in business, no more gold to be mined, no more computers to be invented. As I point out to them, it's not the product that builds a business; it's the person who recognizes the need for the product and makes things happen. Agnes Rolnick saw a need, knew the time was right—and had the guts and persistence to take advantage of the moment.

12

Conclusion: Of Course You Can

If you bought or borrowed this book, you have been thinking of starting your own business. Maybe it's one of those "I must do someday" goals that's been floating around in your head along with the one about losing ten pounds. Perhaps your problem has been trying to figure out what kind of business you feel qualified to handle; in that case, the Skills-You-Can-Sell Conversion Chart should help you find the enterprise that will be right for you. Or could it be that you have a tangible idea you have been wanting to put into action, but are not quite sure how to go about it?

Possibly you have been deterred by sloth, but most likely it's that age-old road block for women who want to enter the male bastion of business management: fear of failure.

Don't let the fear stop you. When I started to learn how to drive a car, I felt I would never learn to master all those complex procedures, and I quaked with nervousness about the impending driver's test. Until one day I started to look at the people behind the wheels of those cars and trucks I saw going by and the thought suddenly hit me: "If all those idiots have learned to drive and pass the test, so can I."

Look around you at the storekeepers and business owners you deal with—are they brilliant? Your next-door neighbor who has built a successful insurance business—does he strike you as a rocket-scientist? You don't have to be a Lee Iacocca or Donald Trump to start and run a profitable business.

All you need is an idea, and the drive and determination to bring it to fruition. To repeat those famous words of Franklin D. Roosevelt, inspired by Henry David Thoreau: "All we have to fear is fear itself."

The purpose of this book is to teach you the rudiments of building a business, to prepare you for the emotional as well as practical factors that will involve and occupy your mind and time, and to reassure you by telling you about other women—no more gifted than you—who have made it. You will work harder and under greater pressure than you ever have, but you will adore every minute of it. The effort is prodigious; it's exhausting but exciting. But when you succeed, it can be one of the most satisfying and rewarding achievements of your life.

Don't hesitate. Don't waiver. You're ready—*GO FOR IT*.

Index